The Spirit of Selling

The 5 Ds of Selling

The Spirit
of
Selling

The 5 Ds of Selling

Nick Savastano

The Spirit of Selling– The 5 Ds of Selling

Published by StreetWise Publications
Suite 1, 22 Waikanda Cres, Whalan, NSW 2770 Sydney, Australia
Copyright Nick Savastano 2013
All Rights Reserved

ISBN: 978-1495230707

© Nick Savastano 2013
Savastano, Nick –

Dedication

This book is dedicated to my wife, Jayne and our three children...

I would also like to note my sincere appreciation to all of my clients, friends and the sales professionals I have interacted with. This book has been drawn from our joint experience.

Table of Contents

Foreword

'The Spirit of Selling – The 5 Ds of Successful Selling', is Nick Savastano's approach to selling, successfully. Written in an entertaining yet educational 'parable' style, the story follows the experiences of a financial services salesman, 'Nick' and his training under the tutelage of sales expert, Pele Sarsson. Nick's journey of enlightenment into the world of successful selling is one I experienced before I left the world of professional selling and focused on writing, publishing and editing. Yet I still sell every day of my life, as do we all.

Everyone must be a salesperson as well as an expert in whatever service they offer, or product they sell. The lessons learned by 'Nick' in his time with Pele can be used by all of us, no matter what we sell or do. The focus is on the customer and that is always the key to getting the business.

Some of us have a less than laudatory opinion of sales people, not always drawn from first hand experience but everyone would have their own 'horror' story of being sold something that was not what we really wanted, or needed, or as described on the box. Some even equate sales people with con men. A con man is a confidence trickster, someone who gains the confidence of their mark and then cheats them. A sales person gains the confidence of their customer, then gives them value.

The Spirit of Selling demonstrates how sales people can gain the confidence and trust of their prospect, it discusses the art or 'philosophy' of seling. The 'science' is in the *'5Ds of Successful Selling'*; how to service their needs accurately and give them value. Then come back and do it again and again and service their friends, relatives, colleagues and peers. Referrals and repeat business is extremely valuable if only because the time, effort and expense of attracting new business is minimized or done away with completely. You will never get referrals or repeat business if you don't have the confidence and trust of your client and, you will never have that if you don't sell to them professionally, with their needs always at the forefront. This book tells you exactly how to achieve this.

The 5 Ds; *Discovery, Dialogue, Direction, Decision and Delivery* are explained in a way that everyone can understand and then apply, no matter what kind of selling they do. Business to business, retail, professional services, big ticket items, FMCGs... it makes no difference because the method can be adapted to suit the selling process you follow. For those who must find their prospects and then obtain an appointment, present their service or product and overcome objections (as opposed to someone who responds to clients walking into their showroom or office more or less unbidden), the 5 Ds will make prospecting and cold calling a joy as well as a stimulating challenge. For those who sell to a 'captive audience' but must compete with some serious opposition (luxury cars, lawyers, orthodontists, stock brokers etc), the 5 Ds will make the difference between a 'Yes' and a 'Maybe'.

I know you will enjoy this book and please, feel free to contact the author if you have any comments, queries or would like to discuss with Nick what you enjoyed about the book and which parts really made an impact on you and your personal approach to selling.

Perry Gamsby, D.Lit., MA(Writing), Dip. Business, Dip. Marketing
Editor, StreetWise Publications
Email: streetwise@gmail.com
January 2014

Chapter 1 Discovery

'There is no better High than Discovery'
E.O.Wilson

It was early morning. My iPhone's alarm function was lighting up the bedside cabinet, the fluorescent light arguing with the familiar alarm tune as to which would get my attention. I decided to call it a draw and tapped the snooze option. I knew I'd need the extra fifteen minutes to get going, yet as my feet strayed to the cold side of the bed I quickly rolled back into the warm patch I had slept the night in and stared at the ceiling. Wide awake.

My mind was already starting to race with thoughts, mostly just general feelings of anxiety. Today I was to meet a sales coach that had been sent by the company to help improve my sales results. I'm a regional sales executive with a major firm in the marketplace. I'm the first to admit I was in a rut and my sales weren't what they should be despite it having been a tough year all round.

My motivation had been really tested this year and it just seemed to continue to get worse and worse for me. I was now really questioning whether I was cut out for this career in sales. I jumped out of bed after my third time at hitting the snooze button. I jumped in the shower and as the warm water tickled the back of my head I started to think about how do I get the motivation to even go in today?

After showering, shaving and throwing on my best suit I left my apartment, still undecided about actually making it to work. I just couldn't come up with a plausible excuse I could live with. As I stood waiting at the elevator, which generally takes an age to reach the 38th floor, my mind started worrying about what kind of day I would have. I wondered whether I would get fired if he reports that I am not up to this sales role. This day is going to be a long one I thought.

It was the ping of the elevator arriving that broke my thoughts. The cab journey into the office was slow as we weaved through the traffic, the only joy on the journey was it was a sunny day and the light streamed through the window onto my face as I watched the landmarks passing by. Arriving in the office with plenty of time to spare, I was greeted by Jane the receptionist.

"Hey Nick! I thought you were meeting Pele today ?"

"I am" I replied.

"Well what are you doing here?" The sudden realisation that I might be in the wrong place washed over me, with the same unstoppable force the sea washes over a small pebble on the beach. The similarity of my insignificance in this process hit home just as the little voice in my head started with the profanities. The Anglo-Saxon expletives slipped out before I asked "Where am I meant to be then?"

Jane looked at me and laughed. "Don't you read your emails?"

"Of course I do."

"Then why are you asking?" Good question, I thought, as I fumbled for my Blackberry in the inside pocket of my suit. She interrupted my fumbling with "He is in head office and his office is on the management floor."

"Thanks" I said as I dashed off. I got to the lift, pressed the down button and as the old saying goes, 'More haste less speed', the lift took ages to come, then stopped on every floor going down. I ran outside and fortunately there was a cab waiting. It was only a ten minute drive from the sales office to the head office. I signed in at security and again dashed to the elevators. As I walked into the reception on the management floor, I noticed the carpets had changed. They were thick pile and deep red in colour, the receptionist asked me if she could help. I said, "Yes. I was due to meet Pele Sarsson at 9am". As we both looked up at the bank of clocks on the wall from various countries, I could see I was 20 minutes late. Two minutes later I was told to go into his office which was located at the end of the corridor. I walked across the carpet sinking with each step, not only into the pile but into my string of excuses for being late.

The door was open and I could smell the aroma of fresh coffee coming from the office. I put my head around the door and got my first sight of Pele standing there, looking out of the floor to ceiling glass windows at the view across the city. The sun streamed into the room causing an almost halo effect to surround him as he stood there. I coughed and said "Can I come in?"

Without looking around he said; "I don't know Nick, can you? More importantly, do you want to?"

I froze at the door for a split second and said "Yes, to both."

He turned around and smiled and I felt the sincerity in it. "Good answer and if i was here to judge, I would say it was the right one. Take a seat Nick, would you like a coffee?"

"That would be great" I said. He walked around and poured it for me.

"Milk and sugar?"

"Yes please, one sugar and milk, thank you."

He put my coffee down on the coffee table in front of me and sat down on the sofa opposite. He looked straight at me and said; "Why are you here Nick?"

"I was told to come by my manager."

"So if you hadn't been told to come, what would you be doing differently?"

"I don't understand?"

"Well, as your performance this year is way below your best, I wondered what you would be doing differently if you hadn't been told to come?"

I was about to get defensive, however I just blurted out, "I'm not sure."

"Well, Einstein said 'to continually do the same process and expect a different result is insane'. Just so I know what I am dealing with, are you insane Nick?"

We both laughed. "I am many things but I don't think I am insane."

"Well Nick, we will deal with the many things you and are not later in the session. Good, so Nick, what do you want to get out of us working together today?"

"Actually I have not really thought about it."

"How often do you go to meetings without a set agenda or at least having a set objective?"

"About 50% of the time I suppose," knowing it was probably a much bigger percentage.

He just looked at me warmly. "So what you are saying is, part of your sales process allows you to do half of your meetings by the seat of your pants and the other half in a structured way?"

"Umm, yes I suppose so."

"So, how do you decide which process goes with which prospect or client meeting, Nick?"

I sat there thinking for a second, feeling it was a trick question. "I don't decide as such, I make the appointments and go along with the intention of selling."

"Therefore what you are really saying is that your actual process is at best a loose process that works on the basis that your personality will sell the product?"

"Yes. Is selling not about personality?"

"That is an interesting question Nick. Is selling based on 'personal or professional equity? Another way to say that and one I like to use, is to recognise selling, unlike lots of professions, is an art and a science. The science being the actual sales process and the art is like the wind that blows through the long grass it fills the process with You. So Nick, you are the wind in the process but not the process, do you understand?"

I was inwardly focused for a second thinking about the long grass, blowing in the wind. My mental image of the billowing green grass was almost hypnotic. I felt myself come back to consciousness. "Yes. I think so. What you are saying is, that I can't operate without a process no matter how great a personality I am."

"Yes Nick, you can't operate without a sales process. I am happy to accept you are a great personality by the way, as to a great salesman, that's for you to prove to yourself, as my presumption is that you are. Let me ask you another question Nick."

"Sure."

"When you go to a sales meeting do you normally take a pen and notebook?"

"Yes of course."

"Why do you do that?"

"To take notes of course." The penny had already dropped. This was a polite and constructive bollocking and only 5 minutes into the meeting things were looking up. I fumbled in my jacket pocket on the left hand side, nothing. The little voice started again with the profanities, then the sweating, then I tried the right side pocket, still nothing. The feeling of censure was on its way. I knew it, as I had been here before. I placed my note pad of the table and looked up. Pele was just looking at me, smiling, with a pen in his outstretched hand. "Thank you" I said as I took it and opened the note book.

"It is only a suggestion Nick, however, so you and I can get the most out of the day, please take notes, reflect on what I say, challenge me, take the bits that work and use them with my blessing. The bits that don't work, adapt them. Just one good idea that turns your performance around is worth all my time and more importantly worth all your time. So to summarise so far, what have you learned apart from the fact I make great coffee?"

"You do make great coffee Pele, thank you." I sat and reflected, something I hadn't done for a while due to my rushing around trying to hit targets in my downward spiral of desperate activities. I wrote:

Selling is:
Art and a Science
Personality alone will not sell any thing, you need both Personality and a Sales Process. There is a difference between personal and professional equity in relationships, Know your Outcomes or Objectives of the call.

"Perfect Nick; don't forget, to write something down you need both a pen and a note pad! You hang on to the pen for today. I glanced down at it and noticed it was a Mont Blanc; nice pen, I thought. "Thank you."

"Nick, I want to discuss the first part of my 5D sales model which I call Discovery. The reason I call it Discovery is because there are two main elements that make up this critical section that considers discovery of oneself, which I call the internal landscape, and discovery of your clients, which I call the external landscape. So as you wrote down selling is an art and a science, let me expand that for our discussion, is that Ok?"

"Yes, that's fine with me."

"So first the internal part will look at some guiding principles and what I call sales presuppositions. These are true for me and they are principles that change the way I think and interact with clients. The first part of discovery is the realisation we are all part of a greater system and how we interact with that greater system effects the outcomes we have both in life and in sales."

I listened intently, as I was struggling to follow what Pele meant. I must have looked perplexed as he said; "I can sense you are not with me on this point yet Nick, so let me put it into a useable and understandable context. Nothing that you ever think, say, or do is ever in isolation. It is not in isolation internally or externally." At this stage I was totally lost, I was almost drowning it was so deep. "Our first experience of each other was when?"

"Here, this morning" I said.

"Were you on time?"

"Ummm… No, I was late."

"Why were you late?"

"I didn't fully read my email notice about the meeting."

"How did you feel about being late?"

"Actually, really annoyed, and under pressure."

"Is this a good place to start a sales meeting?"

"No".

"So internally, as in your mind, that little voice is telling you, you are in the wrong mental space. It is expending mental energy on you rather than me and the meeting. Your focus is inward not outward."

I just sat there and listened to him talk. His voice was almost hypnotic, like the wind blowing through the reeds again, except it was my mind that he was now moving. I was struggling with my consciousness, I was almost in a trance trying to process this and reflect at the same time.

"Now Nick, how about me?"

"What do you mean?"

"Well I am part of the same system am I not?"

"I am not sure I relate?"

" Well you are having a meeting with me, are you not?"

"Sure."

"How do I perceive the fact you are late to our first meeting?"

"Yes, sure, I understand that."

"Do you really? Do you really understand the real implications of this connection between you and I Nick?"

I just looked at him. It felt he was looking deep into my soul, it felt as if he could see all my truths and lies laid out on the table in front of him.

"Nick the sales process is a contextual sphere, what you do at point one has a direct correlation on what happens at point two. Nothing is in isolation, you are never outside that sphere. Your being late may be a simple example however, it shows that there is a cause and effect model working all the time. Write this down in your book Nick."

Results Versus Reasons.

"See Nick, you were late and you will internalise and justify why you were late, yet validity is not yours. The other part of the system is me and let's say I am really annoyed by people who are late. Where are we on a scale of 1-10 on great starts? More importantly and let's say I follow the result vs reasons model, I could say, 'Hey, I have listen to your reasons (excuse) Nick of why you were late and I say sorry Nick I don't accept it so, actually I don't want to deal with you thanks'. This model, Nick, should be ingrained across the whole of your mental conditioning. Write this;"

You are totally responsible for your results and if you don't get the results you want its your Fault

"I don't know whether that is true Pele" I said. "What happens if the reason is outside your control?"

"Good question Nick. When you say true, you mean it isn't true to you personally. In other words, you are struggling to accept the assertion that you could have that much power over the sales process."

I have to say, it did cross my mind when Pele mentioned the model earlier that my blaming everything else and or anyone else, is a lot easier than this model. I said, "Yes, but I don't set my sales targets, what happens if they are set too high? How do I hit the target?"

"Nick, let's say we create a Model right now to deal with this, would that be useful?"

"Sure that would be useful."

"Take my pen and draw a circle in the centre write **CONTROL**. Now around that circle, draw a larger circle and in that write **CANNOT CONTROL**."

"Okay, let's now look at the point you made earlier ,about your target. Which Circle does it sit in according to you?"

"It sits in the Cannot Control circle."

"Notice how the Control circle is central to the model and the outer circle clearly has influence but is not central?"

"I see that" I said.

"So your argument and thought process is that someone else has control over you and your sales process by allocating a number to you right?"

"Well I didn't quite see it like that when I said it, but yes I suppose."

"Okay, let's just stick with it for the moment if we can. So let's say we cannot control the target setting process; what can we control?"

"I am not sure."

"Nick I want you to imagine you we're able to sit in the control circle now, what would you say?"

"I would say my activities control the quantity and the quality of those activities to hit the target."

"That's Excellent Nick! I would write that down as an important point in what I call the Discovery section of the sales model.

I can control the Quantity the Quality of all my Activities.

"The other part of control is interesting, Nick. Did you hear the news today?"

"No, not really Pele. I can't say that I did, why?"

"Kanye West made an interesting comment, he said; 'I am a god'."

"Clearly the guy is a nutter!"

"Yes. The response that everyone made is, exactly that. Or who does he think he is? He is blaspheming."

"What's this got to do with control Pele?"

"Well Nick, the other part of control is creation."

"What do you mean?"

"The world around you has been created by who?"

"I don't know Pele."

"Man? God? Who? Let's start with Man then Nick. The world and the evolution of the planet as we know it, has come from human choices. The world around us is a creation of what Governments believe is best for society. The legislators create laws that society believes is best for the majority. As you know Nick, this leads to misrepresentation of the minorities. Interestingly, politicians are elected by minorities in most societies and at best have a minority view of what is best for us."

"Sorry Pele, but what's this got to do with me and sales?"

"Everything Nick! See, like the politicians, we all have the minority view, yours is the minority of one! The choices you make are self centered and the world around you is the outcome of all your choices! Nick, Kanye West is right, forget whether he actually believes he is a god. The focus of your mind is wrong.

The concept of our ability to create the world around us through our choices is scary. You could argue we have god like powers. If you knew you had the power to create whatever you wanted, if you could control your thinking and hence your choices Nick, what would you differently in your sales career, in fact your life, Nick?"

I was still mulling this over and he took my silence as license to continue.

"So the fundamental part of Control is your thinking and the realisation that if you focus long enough you can create a different world around you. Write this down; Better Thoughts, Better Words, Better Actions."

Better Thoughts, Better Words, Better Actions

I looked up when I finished jotting that down and Pele handed me a poem written by a woman called Marianne Williamson. It began...

Our deepest fear is not that we are inadequate.
Our deepest fear is that we are powerful beyond measure.
It is our light, not our darkness
That most frightens us.

As I read this, emotion started to well up inside me, a feeling of being able to achieve anything I wanted washed over me. I looked at Pele and all he said was, "You can achieve anything Nick, don't let your thinking stop you." There was silence in the room as we shared that moment of my realisation of how powerful I could be if I just chose to be so. Then Pele spoke.

"Nick a question for you."

"What's is it, Pele?"

"Reality."

"I don't understand?"

"Well when you meet a client or prospect, whose reality are you approaching the meeting from?"

"My own, I suppose."

"Whose reality is the most important?"

"Well my instinct says the client's."

"Nick, the important thing is to realise that your reality is not reality itself, it is just your reality. Client understanding is about understanding their reality, without imposing your reality on theirs. This seems simple, however it is difficult as most sales people push their own reality on to the client through product. This brings us to an important guiding principle and to the next presupposition. Your reality is not reality itself, just your reality,"

So as I wrote it down in my notepad, I started thinking, is that right? Surely, that's not true?

Your Reality Is Not Reality Itself Just Your Reality

"Sorry Pele, that can't be right. I must tell the customer what is right from the company's point of view or as you say, reality. Also, I am there to sell so I must tell the customer about my products and or services."

"Okay Nick, let me answer your question and expand it in the sales context in line with this guiding principle. The starting point is; Telling Is Not Selling, Nick."

I wrote that down, too.

Telling Is Not Selling

"Your question is interesting because it builds on two questions sales people always ask me all the time. Firstly, the guiding principle is an underlying philosophy that puts you in the perceptual position of the client. Do you know the saying, 'walk a mile in someone else's shoes'?"

"Yes, sure."

"In other words Nick, and specifically in a sales context, when people talk about consultative selling, it's not just about asking questions, you know that, right?"

"Well actually, if I am truthful Pele, I thought it was just that. Asking lots of open questions, so that I can just tailor my products better to the clients needs."

"That is an interesting statement, Nick. So selling to you, is about linguistic sleight of mouth through questioning, so you can get a list of needs you then push a product against?"

"Well I suppose so, but I have been on consultative sales programs and that is pretty much it in my experience."

"Okay Nick, come back to me, I sense you are getting yourself into the wrong mental space. Focus on the underlying philosophy. Is understanding the client a good thing?"

"Of course it is."

"Good. Now understanding a customer may come linguistically from asking questions, however, your wanting to understand the customer and build a meaningful relationship with him or her is something else. Nick, I fundamentally believe that the sales process cannot be separated from the individual. The guiding principles are what make the difference from doing a sales job, or being a great sales person. In much grander context, wanting to have great relationships generally is a belief system, it is in your DNA. This builds on the second point, Nick. Ask yourself a question. Have you met anyone you don't like?"

"Yes loads of times Pele."

"So why didn't you like them?"

"I suppose I didn't like what I saw, or they said or did something I didn't like."

"So you judged them, given a set of criteria you have mentally created right?"

"Well yes, but we all do that!"

"Does that make it right to judge someone by your own criteria, Nick? That's like saying, 'do you know what, I've always done things this way so the idea of change to me is just a mental concept as I am not changing'. Yet whether we accept change or not, it is happening, it is a reality that doesn't need our acceptance. Why do I say that? Because the next guiding principle is, write this down, we are in constant rapport but it is neutral."

Rapport Is Constant But Neutral

"Before you judge this guiding principle Nick, let me continue as it ties into the second point. We believe this cannot be true because we all know people we don't like. However, if I recognise that unless I judge their behaviour against a set of self imposed values, I might actually start from a different place. See Nick, this guiding principle and the 'reality is not reality itself' principle sets a level of thinking that makes us want to build relationships. It makes us want to listen and learn about our prospects and clients. There are so many great people out there, why limit yourself to people that are exactly the same as you. Dolly the sheep might be cloned, but try to be Nick, not Dolly."

"The second part that relates to your question and the question I get asked the most about at this point is structure of the sales call. The science is the process, the 1,2,3,4,5 of selling. So when do you tell? When do you listen? When do you ask probing questions? These are all structural meeting questions, which I will talk about later when you are ready. We have the whole day Nick, don't look like I have just upset you by inferring you're not ready. Another important life and sales lesson Nick is ego. Don't let it cloud your thinking. Recognise it when it shows up like now."

I just sat there listening, he was right, ego did enter my thinking, in fact almost an aggressive ego that made me think I will show him who is ready. Yet he seemed to just disarm me by recognising it in me.

"Nick I suggest we take a quick break, but before we do that did you bring the 100 prospects' names and numbers I asked for?"

I reached into my trouser pocket and pulled out the list of 100 names and handed them to him. "Here we go Pele. I wasn't sure why you needed them or in what format."

"Any format works as it will be you ringing them later today to set up meetings for us to go to together."

I now needed a toilet break, my body temperature was rising and the little voice was working at a hundred miles an hour on my excuses... between the profanities. Pele looked at me, smiling. He smiled the smile that said he knew what was going on in my head. The 'result versus reasons' principle popped into my head at this point. I knew now exactly what he meant.

When I returned to Pele's office after my visit to the bathroom and a longer than usual period of the customary mirror staring, I did seem calmer inside, even with the realisation that I was going to be on the phone cold calling my list of prospects.

"Nick tell me about the list."

"What do you mean" I asked as I was playing for time.

"How did you get the list?"

"Well, from cards I picked up around some events, some mates, and the rest are from the phone book."

He nodded at the mention of each source, then said, "Before we get into ringing them, lets discuss how you normally get your prospects."

"I was told always to be prospecting, so I chat to people when I am out; in bars, clubs at the gym etcetera."

"How is that working for you?"

"Yes, it's okay."

"When you say it's okay, what are your call ratios? Nick, how many meetings do you get from being out socially prospecting?"

"I don't know to be honest. I collect the cards and then try to make meetings the following day. Some days it's good, some days it's not."

"Okay Nick, how many cards do you need to collect to get a meeting?"

"I am still not certain Pele, say 10 to 15 cards gives me a meeting. Competition is tough Pele!" As I said this, 'Results versus Reasons' popped back into my head. It was like it was now anchored to all my excuses.

"Nick how many meetings are you doing a week?"

"Five meetings per week I suppose."

"How many sales are you doing per week out of those 5 meetings?"

"Some weeks none, some weeks one."

"So to summaries this then, Nick, your sales strategy for obtaining qualified, high quality prospects, is to go to bars, nightclubs and gyms. To obtain business cards from 40-60 people per month and then get 20 of them to agree to meet you

again. Then when you do meet these like-minded social butterflies, your passion for your product and ability to build
credibility, trust and maintain rapport means that on average,
two of them per month say 'Yes'. Nick, you know what I said
earlier about insanity and you said, 'I am many things but I am
not insane', I have to say Nick, I now need convincing."

I was now feeling beaten up. When Pele described my prospecting method like that I realised the whole approach sounded
just as he insinuated, insane. How do I now respond? It's totally
in my control I know. I wanted to respond defensively, blame
my manger for telling me to do it this way, yet something inside
me kept saying, take responsibility and not the blame. Before I
got a chance to say anything, Pele began to speak in his precise,
hypnotic style.

"Nick, we have known each other for nearly two hours now.
Do you feel you can trust me?"

Strangely, I did. I didn't believe he would, go behind my back
and give me a bad company review about my performance. I
trusted him. "Yes, Pele I do trust you" I said and I meant it sin-
cerely.

"And do you believe that I have your best interests at heart?"

"Yes I think so. Yes, I do."

"Then good because in this environment there is no failure,
only feedback." I scribbled that down as he said it.

No Failure, Only Feedback!

"When I say there is no failure only feedback, Nick, it doesn't
really matter what your ratios are. They are only ratios. What
matters is what those ratios mean to you."

"Well they didn't mean anything as I wasn't aware of them,
because I wasn't tracking them."

"See the beauty of this process is consciousness, 'now I am
lost Pele' and 'then you are found Nick'. I mean, you are now
aware of the ratios and how do you feel about them now, right
this second?"

"I feel like sh… excrement, if I am honest."

"Do you like feeling like 'excrement', Nick?" he smiled at my attempt to keep the language on a professional level.

"No I hate it."

"So we have established that what you're doing presently makes you feel like, excrement. Why are you feeling that specifically?"

"Because I am not making sales and I want to succeed."

"Nick, so there is the feedback. You want to succeed; what you are doing now is moving you away from success, not towards it. All we have to do is change what you are doing. Failure, Nick. With failure you are empowered to change and become successful and I will help you."

It was not what I expected. I was mentally feeling amazed, empowered. It was like Pele had got into my head and shook all the sh… excrement out of it. I sat in silence for a minute staring down at the note pad. No Failure, only Feedback!

Pele broke my self imposed trance. "Nick, I was just wondering, as you sat there, what are you experiencing right now?"

"Experiencing? I am not sure Pele. I suppose I am having a realisation how important not being reactive in my life is and also in my sales role."

"So what's the difference between being reactive and proactive, Nick?"

"I suppose, one is responding, the other is getting out in front of the event, I would say Pele."

"Yes, reactive is looking into the past and responding, proactive is looking out into the future and predicting what will happen. It's time for us to talk about experience generally, before we experience a sales meeting together. For us to really understand how a client will respond to our telephone calls and our sales approach in the meeting, we have to experience how they respond to our approach. You can only know what it feels like to make a cold call when you make one. The experience you get when a client says no to you is experiential. We can read as many books as we wish, we can watch instructional videos from the 'gurus', but experience from doing, that leads to understanding and creates a real feedback loop for us."

I wrote down;

My Understanding Only Comes From Experience

"Nick, I think of it as C.O.R.D. The reason why I think of it in this context is because C.O.R.D. means an influence, feeling, or force that binds or restrains; a bond or tie. Experience is the bond between us all. We are the sum total of our experiences. Our relationships are also the some total of those experiences. Nick, to be a great salesman you need to go out and get the most experience you can from each interaction. Write this down, Nick. C.O.R.D. means:"

Concrete experience,
Observation(internal reflection)
Re-apply learning, (adapt to personal context)
Do it again (Create new Experience)

"Nick, this leads us to the process part, of what I call the external elements of Discovery. This is the process the science. So Nick, get out your list and let's look at ringing a few people."

The butterflies in the stomach started as I got out the piece of paper. It was an Excel spreadsheet with the names of my prospects with their numbers on it. As Pele reminded me earlier, it was the collation of business cards from my socialising in bars and clubs. Either way, I was committed to trying to get the most out of them.

Pele asked me to come over and sit behind the desk and use his Phone. As I walked over to sit down he asked me whether I normally used a script when I was calling? I said, "I don't use one, should I?"

"Actually Nick it depends on how fluid the call is?"

"Fluid? What do you mean?"

"Well, as long as it flows smoothly, also, you know what the objective of the call is? Don't mumble or let the prospect take control, it will be fine not to have a script."

Oh well this will be fun I thought, knowing sometimes I do fumble my way through the call. This of course is made worse when the prospect is difficult, or starts objecting to me calling him or her. I sat down and made my self comfortable, placed the paper down and looked at the phone. With an internal sigh I picked up the handset. Just as I started to punch the numbers Pele spoke.

"Nick, just one second."

I looked at him, he was still smiling when he pushed the receiver button down, to cut the line off. "Nick, where is my pen?"

"What?"

"My pen?"

I took the pen out of my pocket and went to hand it to him.

"No Nick, how will you take notes and write down your appointments without it?"

"I would have taken it out when I made one" I said.

"Nick, it is about planning and preparation now, this is about the process. It is about creating the right frame of mind that allows you to make as many appointments as you can in the shortest time possible. Fumbling around getting your diary out, looking for a pen is an amateur process. In fact Nick, I read an interesting article written by Boshoff and Arnolds where they identified that the correct utilisation of time and energy at the task at hand and how well a person takes actions towards completing their work tasks leads to better job performance."

"Also Nick , there was an article published online with O*NET by Farr and Trippins in 2010 where they acknowledged telesales competences. I've got a print out of it here, let me read it to you."

More specifically, it is of great importance to have the required knowledge in fundamental sales and marketing principles. The required skills that were identified for sales occupations include being able to persuade others to change their minds, being able to communicate effectively, listen actively, actively look for ways to help others and to manage one's own time and the time of other people. Furthermore, it is important to have the ability to communicate information and to speak clearly to others so that they can understand and comprehend the intended message and to comprehend communications from others by listening and understanding.

"So Nick, before you make the call write in your book these headers."

I will persuade and change someone's Mind
I will communicate information clearly and effectively
I will actively Listen
The Prospect will understand the objective of the call and agree to invest the time

"Okay Nick, I think you are ready to make the call. You might need to tweak the mental script as you go but hey, experience will come from the moment the first prospect responds to your communication."

"Okay Pele, I think I am good to go."

"Great!"

It felt like standing at the back of a Hercules C130, tailgate down, Red on, standby, standby, Green on Go! Go! Go! The question was whether Pele would act as my static line and open my chute if it went wrong? I burnt the first three prospects with no joy before Pele stepped in.

"So tell me Nick, what is happening with the calls?"

"Well I keep getting that they are not interested!"

"Write down another point, Nick, that applies to the telephone and when we meet the client or prospect face to face."

You Cannot NOT Communicate

"How does that work?" I said.

"Well Nick the mind cannot do negation. If you say, 'Mr X don't worry about the cost!' What do you think he is now thinking about?"

"Ah, the cost?"

"This is why it is important to keep to the objective of the call and not get sucked into a product discussion on the phone. When I was listening you went straight into the product by saying, 'Mr X I want to talk to you about pensions, your savings, your tax planning etcetera'. What does the client respond to?"

"What I say to him."

"Okay, so he says, 'Thanks but I have my pension sorted out thanks, my savings are taken care of' etcetera. Even if they aren't they will likely say it to you. Why? Because you are a sales guy and not even a referred sales guy."

"So what do I do Pele?"

"Well, as Steve Jobs said, *'Simple can be harder than complex. You have to work hard to get your thinking clean to make it simple. But it's worth it in the end because once you get there, you can move mountains.'* What is the purpose of the call? To make appointments right?"

"Yes."

"So why are you talking about products?"

"The client takes me there."

"No, you take him there with what you say. The client is always responding to what you say, unless he/she takes control of the call and then you are responding to him/her. So let me ask you another question Nick. How long do you need in time from a client?"

"Well Pele, to do a financial review takes an hour."

"There is your first problem. No one is going to give you an hour off the back of a cold call. The time is too long Nick, you might get 10 minutes."

"I can't do my job in 10 minutes, Pele. You don't understand the business."

"Actually Nick, I do understand the business. You need to change your understanding about the structure of the process."

"You need to explain that Pele because I am lost now."

"Okay Nick you need an hour to do a financial review, right?"

"Yes."

"Okay but how do you do that without an appointment?"

"I can't, obviously."

"Right, so I will show you the structure of the first meeting and how to get from ten minutes to 1 hour later. Now you focus on getting the ten minutes."

"I am struggling, what do you suggest?"

"Well, Nick, what is it you do?"

"You know what we do, we are a financial services company."

"What is it you do?"

"I sell financial services products. I don't understand Pele?"

"No Nick, you don't. There was an old saying, 'Sell the sizzle not the steak'. What do your products do?"

"They build wealth for people."

"Okay Nick, that is the starting point. An important point Nick is to realise that:"

Agreement Can Always Be Found At Some Level Of Ambiguity

"How does that work Pele? Can you give me an example?"

"Sure Nick I can. You said you sell financial products, right? And I moved you towards ambiguity, with the 'what is the purpose of your products' question. The products build wealth or help people accumulate wealth is that right? So let's play this out Nick, is that okay?"

"Sure is." Mentally I was thinking this will be fun to watch.

"Hello Nick, I have a new service that helps people accumulate wealth, is that something that would interest you?"

"But Pele! I was always told to ask open questions, that is a closed question".

"Nick, what you say is correct, it is a closed question, not an open one. To use an open one is incorrect in this context. 'Why?', I hear you say. Well, the reason is because part of the sales process is, write this down Nick:"

Gaining Customer Commitment To The Next Step

"So, back to the question Nick. 'I have a service that helps people accumulate wealth; is that something that interests you?' And you say?"

"Well I would say yes, but what happens if they say no?"

"Well Nick, if they say no and mean it, then they are not a prospect. If, however, they say no as resistance to your approach, then you can genuinely say, 'Mr or Mrs X out of all my clients, I have never had anyone say that they are not interested in accumulating wealth, unless they are ultra high net worth clients. As you are not interested in wealth accumulation perhaps I can take ten minutes of your time to talk about wealth preservation? Is Tuesday around 11 am good for you or can you suggest a better time?' Most people say yes. Why? Because most people are trying to accumulate wealth for a whole host of reasons. Now follow the logic Nick. They say yes, they are interested. What do you do next?"

"I suppose I make the appointment."

"Yes, correct, this is where the ten minutes is important Nick because what happens if they still resist? Say they say yes to the accumulation question, you now follow with; 'great, so all I need is ten minutes of your time; is Tuesday good or is another day better for you?' They will say something like 'Nick, tell me about the service.' You respond with, 'well Mr X, wealth accumulation is such a large topic and I only need 10 minutes of your time, what time on Tuesday is best?' Perhaps, more resistance; 'Sure Nick, but what products are you selling?' You need to answer his question without answering it in such a way that you don't upset him but you do secure the ten minutes you need. 'Actually Mr X, as I said, wealth accumulation is such a large topic and without knowing your personal circumstances, and you did say you were interested in accumulating wealth, is Tuesday at 11 good or do you have a time that works better?' Nick, this is why you ask a closed question first. Once you get commitment through the yes it is very difficult for them to then say 'no, actually I changed my mind.' It is also the reason you keep pushing the objective of the appointment of ten minutes. It is only ten minutes isn't Nick? Nick, the thing is, this also works with your socialising in pubs, bars and clubs."

"What do you mean Pele?"

"Well the concept creates a yes, therefore an implied permission to call them the following day. Let me explain, you know when you're in a bar or club, what is the first thing someone asks you?"

"They normally ask me what is it that I do Pele"

"What is it you say to them?"

"I am in Financial services."

"I should get you to read the book *How to Win Friends and Influence People* by Dale Carnegie."

"Why do you say that?"

"Well, I wondered how many left by the nearest exit when you said you were in financial services?"

"To be honest, Pele, when I first started out in financial services as an insurance broker, it happened all the time. I found myself saying things like, 'I am an insurance broker, however I am not like the rest, I do a professional job' etcetera. I was really conscious of the reputation the industry had generally."

"Has your view changed?"

"Well sometimes it can still be a bit of a limiting belief but that's why I say financial services."

"Okay Nick, are the products you sell beneficial to the clients?"

"Yes."

"Do you know you will do a good job for the client?"

"Yes then forget the limiting belief for now. So where we're we, oh yes, the socialising or networking in bars, for which I am still not convinced it is the most productive way to do it. However, it is for you to consider the alternative options such as social networking not socialising, which I am happy to discuss with you throughout the day. Right Nick, so let's imagine the scenario. A person comes up to you in the bar, they say; 'Hi Nick, what is it that you do?' Try the script. You say; 'I help people accumulate or preserve wealth. What is it you do?' They say; 'I do Y' and the focus is back on them and they will go away thinking you are a great guy."

"Yes but Pele, I don't have a card?"

"Well Nick, during the discussion about them the opportunity will come to give them a card. It will also give you a better understanding of whether you want one from them."

"What do you mean?"

"We need to get you to Quality of Activity and away from Quantity of activity."

"What happens Pele, if they give me a card straight away, what do I say then?"

"Yes Nick a dilemma, a situation that creates a need for flexibility in the process. The situations are not ridged things Nick, remember you must be fluid throughout the process."

"The wind thing is coming, I can feel it."

He smiled and said, "you're right Nick, it is the wind thing because it's you that makes the process flow."

It was like a scene from the X files, how did he know I was thinking that?

"So they offer you a card straight away, which in some cultures is actually what will happen. The process remains the same ultimately Nick. So look at the card, the title, the business and proactively say; 'Thank you. Can I call you John?' or what ever the name on the card is. "My name is Nick and I help people accumulate and preserve wealth, what does (name of the company) Do?. However, and more importantly John, what do you do for them?' Nick, see, we are back to the underlying philosophy of wanting to build better relationships. Sales will come from building better relationships with people, and in particular people that want your products. There has to be some level of qualifying at a process level."

"Pele, you still haven't made the appointment in the club or bar?"

"You are right Nick, what you do is conclude your chat with a structural question. 'John it was really interesting talking to you tonight and perhaps I can give you a ring in a few days to catch up?' He is likely to say what? 'Sure Nick give me a call'. So you now have agreement to call. What do you say when you call him? 'Hi John, it's Nick. As I promised to call I would really like to set a time for a coffee and a catch up'. 'Yes, okay Nick, when were you thinking?' 'Tuesday at 11 works for me unless you can suggest a better time?' He says okay to the time."

"But you have not set an agenda to a meeting, Pele. He doesn't know why you are coming, you won't be able to get into the sales process."

"Nick, the trouble with most sales people is they want sales NOW! They forget we are never out of the sphere of selling, we are always selling and influencing people and outcomes by what we think, say and do. You know that now."

"Sales people always say; 'Hey Pele I am doing sales, I am always taught to be closing, doing deals, it's all about making money."

"No Nick, We are creating relationships, if it is right for him, and makes sense, I will use my considerable influencing skills to make him take action to buy the best product for him. I will see him for a genuine meeting and in that meeting, in the context of selling and to answer your question, I will use that meeting as the start of the process. Actually Nick, you believe that your process starts when you open your mouth at the bar. When, actually, you can never do a deal in a bar anyway. So the absolute best outcome you are likely to get at the bar is what?"

"Get his card I suppose." I thought about that then added; "well it is probably to make an appointment, or get permission to call to make an appointment."

"What is the outcome that I have here?"

"An appointment."

"Exactly Nick, so from a sales objective and process point of view, I have done what I have set out to do right?"

"Yes you have".

"Write this down, Nick:"

The Person With The Greatest Number Of Choices In A Given Situation Is Likely To Get The Best Outcome

"See Nick, If you go into a sales meeting with only one outcome in your mind, you might be focused, however, if you don't achieve that particular outcome, then you're in trouble. If, however, you have the mental flexibility to have several outcomes in mind, then it is likely that you will achieve at least one of your outcomes. Right Nick, back to you. I need you to make 15 appointments this week, for us to go and see together."

I look at Pele thinking 'You are having a laugh, that's three times more than I normally do'. Yet I felt a sudden need for praise and recognition from him and an overwhelming need to achieve the 15 meetings.

Pele said, "I have faith in you Nick. You have the script and mental positioning, so now like life itself it is just down to the application of the knowledge. As they say Nick, knowledge and application are not the same thing."

Pele walked out of the room and left me to it. I started making the calls using the agreed script. He was right, people said yes to the question. I then used the 10 minute meeting pitch. It worked a treat. I made five meetings from eight calls. Granted they were the low hanging fruit from my list, however, it gave me more confidence and it was working. I stuck with the momentum that had been created and within 35 minutes I had made all 15 meetings. I was flying now!

When I was a kid there was a program I can't recall the name of. It had a character called Mr Ben and he use to go into a shop to try on a new suit, go into a wardrobe and come out into a new world. Before he went into the wardrobe a shop keeper would appear. The voice over would say; 'as if by magic the shop keeper appeared'. Pele was like the shop keeper, he seemed to appear right as I had made the 15 meetings and I was Mr Ben. I had entered a new world of prospecting. My worry was that the shop keeper also came into the new world, when it was time for Mr Ben to go back to his normal life. I so hoped this was not going to happen to me yet as I was basking mentally in my success.

Pele came in and said, "Nick, I sense you had a good session. Did you get the 15 meetings?"

"Yes, I did" I said. Internally I was feeling proud and seeking recognition. It came.

"That is great Nick, really good job. Nick please close your eyes."

"Why Pele?"

"Nick you said earlier today that you trust me."

"I do."

"Please close your eyes." I did as instructed. "Now picture yourself making those calls again in your minds eye and as you think about that now, recognise whether you are in the picture or looking at yourself in the picture. If you are looking at yourself, then float down into the picture so you are in the picture looking through your own eyes. As you do that, now, is the picture coloured or black and white?"

"Coloured."

"Good, then make those colours really bright. As you run the picture through your mind, notice whether the picture has a frame around it. If it does, take it off so the picture is moving, that's right, make the picture move now and as it does, recognise any sounds you hear, recognise where they are located, turn them up. that's right Nick. Make them louder and as you do that, see the picture, hear the sounds. Now recognise any feelings you are having, recognise where they are located, make them stronger and stronger now and as you do, turn up those feelings, now enjoy that feeling of success. Know that those 15 appointments in your diary are possible anytime, in fact any time you want them. Know that you can create all that internal praise anytime because you are a success now at prospecting. Now take your right hand and grab your left thumb, that's right, hold it tight Nick and squeeze it, that's right. Now as you squeeze your thumb, I want you to remember this thumb represents the first D in the sales model, that's right, Discovery is the first D. As I count back from 3 to 1 you will open your eyes and know that as you squeeze that thumb you will recover your success and everything you have learned so far; 3-2-1."

I felt good as I opened my eyes and it had seemed to have consolidated all the learning from this morning when I was squeezing my thumb. I squeezed it again, to see if it worked, the word **Discovery** came into my mind plus the feelings I now associated with **Discovery.**

"Nick we should take lunch I think, however just to finalise the Discovery piece and to make sure you tie-up the lose ends on the meetings, you should now send an outlook invite or a mail confirming your meeting and time etc. Territory planning is going to be important consideration going forward, especially as your activity builds."

"When you say territory planning, Pele, do you mean I should manage a certain area?"

"Actually Nick, I was thinking about travelling distance between meetings specifically, however, you may find that certain areas are more productive for you because they have certain types of business clients or offices in that area. So login to your account and send out the confirmation emails and lets do lunch."

"Okay Pele, I will be 15 minutes."

"Perfect I will see you at the elevator."

After sending out the confirmation e-mails, I walked towards the elevator where Pele was already waiting, He was chatting to the CEO. As I approached, I started to slow down, not wanting to interrupt the conversation. I was actually thinking I don't want to meet her. I will be embarrassed because she will put two and two together as I am with Pele and know I am having a session with him about my performance. I stopped a few feet away when Pele turned and said, "Nick, come over and meet Angela."

My heart sank. As I approached her, she smiled a warm sincere smile. I couldn't help but be impressed, you could feel her gravitas, it was palpable.

Pele said, "Angela, this is Nick, he is one of our key sales people."

"It is always great to meet my up and coming sales stars. You do know Nick, that your contribution to our success is critical. Without the hard work that you guys do we wouldn't have a business. Please keep up your good work and please, let me know if I can personally do anything to help you."

I was too busy thinking about what to say whilst she was talking to really appreciate the sincerity in the words. So much for active listening! I just blurted out, "Thank you, that would be nice."

She said, "Well gentlemen, I have a conference call but keep up the good work and I am counting on you Nick" as she swept away up the corridor.

"That would be nice", arghhh! I can't believe I said that, she must think, 'what a loser'. It is the sort of thing most people say when they ask a girl out when they are ten.

Pele just smiled as if he knew exactly what I was thinking. As we walked towards the elevator he said, "Nick we will go to a little Italian restaurant around the corner, my treat."

It was about a five minute walk and it was a traditional Italian with the raffia chianti bottles hanging from the ceilings and the tables hiding under red and white checked table cloths.

"Buon pomeriggio, comestai oggi Pele?" said the head waiter.

"Io sono perfetto, vi ringrazio ONU tavolo a debito a favore" said Pele as I watched in amazement.

"il vostro tavolo normale è pronto per voi."

We walked over to the table with me thinking is there anything this guy can't do? We sat down, on what clearly was his normal table. The staff fussed around us and brought a bottle of sparkling water and two menus.

Pele said, "I recommend the Melazane alla Parmigiana followed by the scialatielli **ai** frutti di mare, the fresh fish is excellent and it is a good Neapolitan dish."

"Sounds good to me", I said, really having absolutely no idea what I had just agreed to eat.

Pele ordered and then said, "Right Nick, so when we go back to the office, we will do a few role plays for the first part of the sales meeting. It is important that we practice that first ten minute structure, before we go out and meet the prospects you have just made appointments with."

"Okay" I said, "that will be great" trying hard to sound enthusiastic.

"You said earlier that you have been on a consultative selling course didn't you?"

"Yes" I said, "but it has been a while," knowing by saying that, if I am rubbish at the role playing I can say I did say it had been a while!

"A while Nick, what is a while?"

"Well at least a year, maybe longer."

"That seems to be a pre frame for failure Nick."

"I don't understand," knowing it was.

"Well I sense you are positioning yourself that if you do badly you will just say you are rusty. I would rather you say; 'Pele I am rusty yet, I will be excellent when we practice'."

Rinsed again! Why am I constantly allowing my negativity to wash through my thinking? "You are right ! I will be great in the role plays and to be truthful, I hate role plays."

"The truth is always the best starting point Nick. Look Nick, in Malcolm Gladwell's book *The Outliers'* he identifies that we must all practice for at least 10,000 hours to attain a level of mastery."

I sat listening, thinking, 'wow that's a long time'. I was worried about the afternoon role play and it probably showed.

"So if we say that's five years of dedicated practice Nick, do you have what it takes to remain focused and dedicate yourself to becoming a master?"

I sat there without replying, I really had to consider whether I had what it took to really dedicate my self to mastery. I started to inwardly focus and visualise what it would take. It would have been easy to say yes, however my concern was life would get in the way. I would need to change my whole approach to my whole life. I mentally saw the words 'discipline' and 'self control' appear in my head. Could I create the self control and discipline that it required to achieve mastery?

Pele just sat in silence waiting for my answer. I was still pondering the question of discipline when he just said; "Nick, 'every man that striveth for mastery is temperate in all things'."

"What does that mean Pele?"

"Well in this context, self control and self discipline are critical in life and in sales. See Nick, self control is a decision, yet perseverance in self control is a different way of thinking all together. To find mastery in all things and in this case sales, is impossible without perseverance in self control. So in simple terms Nick, as you strive for mastery in sales, if you can't remain persistent in your thoughts and control them, mastery will elude you and your performance will be mediocre, as will your life."

I felt the feeling of sadness starting to come over me again as I inwardly reflected. The realisation that lack of self control and self discipline had lead to so many mistakes in my life and my career. Pele was right, I knew that in sales, without the persistence, I would struggle with the knock backs and rejection that is an every day occurrence in sales.

I looked down at the San Pellegrino water that was being poured into the glass next to me. I could hear the fizz bubbling through my thoughts; it didn't break the visual images in my mind until the waiter placed the starter on the table in front of me.

"Nick, You seem to be miles away in your own little reality."

I was still stuck with the reflection of how I would do things differently if I could do it all again. "No Pele I'm here" I said with a half smile.

"Yes Nick, in body."

"No really, Pele I am". I tried to discard the negative feelings, as I refocused on Pele and the lunch. The taste of the starter was good, the smell of fresh basil was enough to change the feelings as I smiled at him and at the little pungent green leaves in front of me.

"So Nick, when we go back to the office we will do the role plays and I will play the client. I would like you to think of the true scenarios you face in the opening part of the meetings. This, however, can wait until we have finished lunch, as all work and no play makes Nick a boring lad." My sentiments exactly I thought. "Nick, tell me a little about your interests and what you normally get up to on the weekends."

I chatted away all over lunch, I don't think he got a word in edge ways. As I got up to leave I suddenly realised he hadn't said very much at all, I still didn't know anything about Pele. He had asked all the questions and I was off on my life's story which he kept flowing through more questions. No wonder I had found the conversation interesting, it was me that had done all the talking. I think I had just had a demonstration of how to maintain a conversation with a customer in a way that was natural.

We left the restaurant and headed back to the office. As we arrived big Hal, as he was known, was just coming out of the revolving doors. I didn't know his surname or at least how to spell it, it was something like Dacfooss or something like that. He walked straight over to Pele and shock his hand. Pele was smiling as he approached him. All I knew about Hal was he was earning at least a million dollars a year and had been the best salesman globally for us every year since I had been there. He was really excited and for a guy in his late thirties, he was bouncing.

"Hi Pele, I tried out that new questioning structure you gave me, it works brilliantly. I am certain it helped me close the two deals this morning."

Pele smiled and said, "I am certain it was your application within the structure, Hal, that made the difference. Either way I am happy that you used it and even more happier that it created such a great experience for you."

Hal was laughing as he walked away; he looked at me and didn't say a word, just smiled a smug sort of 'I love you Pele' grin. as he walked off, still laughing. We went through the revolving doors, strolled across the foyer and arrived at the lifts. Pele pushed the button and we stood there waiting for the bell to announce the lift had arrived. I was hoping he would say something, something encouraging, like 'Nick one day you could be like him'. Instead we just stood there in silence.

I couldn't resist it any longer, my ego needed feeding. "Pele do you think I will be like Hal?"

He just looked straight into my eyes, the warmth was still there. "No Nick you cannot not be like Hal."

My balloon just burst, I was actually shocked by this comment.

He then said, "Nick, the trouble with most people is they are not happy with what they have. They are constantly wishing they were someone else. Just as you wished you were Hal. In reality you look at certain aspects of Hal's life and want it, of course mainly the material things and certainly the good things he has. What happens if I told you Hal has battled with his health for years, would you still want to be Hal?" I was now feeling gutted for what I said. "Well actually Nick, he is perfectly healthily, however your mental frame just changed. Be grateful for what you have and be the best you can be every day. Let others want to be you, Nick, so you can tell them what I just told you. More to your point Nick, the other reason you can't be like Hal is because as I said this morning, you are the wind that blows through the process. You can be like Hal by working hard on the process and practicing. However, it is your individuality that fills the gap of the process, the real you that will create success. Be yourself. Remember, and this is a respectful comment, the problem with most sales managers is just that, that they are managers of the process and because they have success and experience they believe it should always be done their way. Yes it should, but only the process, what actually happens is they try to create clones, 'mini me's'. When you lose your individuality in the process you will fail! You will be someone else and the insincerity will wash over onto the client or prospect." We arrived at the floor. "In these role plays Nick, be yourself."

We exited the elevator and walked to his office, passing the receptionist who smiled and said, "I have blocked the conference room for the whole afternoon Pele."

He thanked her, then opened the door of the conference room, switched on the lights and walked to the far end, checking the flip chart, pens and paper as I stood still in the door way. It was almost like waiting to be invited into someone's house.

"What are you waiting for Nick? No invites here, sit down and get your game head on."

I placed his pen and my notepad down on the table just as the electric blinds were raising, revealing the big expanse of glass that looked right over the bustle of the city.

"Right Nick, what I need you to do is use your imagination and imagine I am one of those meetings you havè set up for us, however it only has to be the initial first 10 minutes. Can you do that?"

Sure, I can I do it every day I thought. "Sure" I said.

"Right, I will give you 15 minutes to prepare but let me leave you with Confucius. 'Success depends upon previous preparation, and without such preparation, there is sure to be failure'."

I watched Pele leave the room as I thought about the Chinese bloke's wisdom before my thinking drifts back to how I'd better get a wiggle on and prepare then.

Chapter 2 Direction

'No solution can ever be found running in three directions'
Deepak Chopra

Pele left the room and I sat there preparing what I would say. In reality I never did this normally, I just winged it. I sat there contemplating both what to say and why I never did it outside of role plays. I scribbled my thoughts down in no logical order as they came into my head. Pele returned, five minutes is never long when you are under pressure.

"Are you ready Nick?"

"Sure."

"Great, go out and come in and as if you were entering my office."

I walked to the back of the room and knocked on the door of the boardroom.

"Come in."

I walked towards Pele who stood up as I approached. I said, "hello my name is Nick and we spoke on the phone."

"Yes, how are you? Please take a seat."

"Thank you." I sat down, then silence. A real pregnant pause as Pele just looked at me and waited. I tried to regain the initiative with, "you have a really nice office here and a great view."

"Yes it is a good view."

More silence.

"Pele, the reason I am here today is to look at how I can help you with your financial planning. When we spoke on the phone you said you would be interested in having a chat."

"That's correct Nick. I am interested in chatting about what you have to offer."

"Great, so for me to understand what would be helpful do you mind if I ask you a few questions?"

"Sure Nick, fire away."

"Pele, how long have you worked here?"

"A long time Nick, so long I can't remember. Okay Nick, stop for a second. How is this going?"

"I think it is going reasonably well."

"Well if the meeting is going to last just ten minutes you'd better build some interest for me."

I now knew it was not going great at all! "Pele you will need to tell me how to do that, I seem to be losing the flow."

"Yes Nick, you have lost the flow and now it feels that you are the proverbial fish out of water. Let's go back to the beginning, remembering that you only have ten minutes to build enough interest so the client will extend the meeting for you."

"I don't know how to do that Pele."

"Let me explain why I consider the first part of the sales call as 'direction'. Write that down."

I scrabbled for pen and paper and added it to my notes.

Direction

"It's like being a movie director Nick, you have to control the set whilst getting the best out of the actors. It is through excellent communication and interpersonal skills built on a solid structure that you control the set and get the best outcome. So the first thing is back to structure. Jot down 'me, us, you'."

Me Us You

"Example. 'Mr X, Thank you for taking time out of your schedule and for seeing me today. As I said on the phone, I will take only ten minutes of your time to talk about wealth accumulation. What I would like to do is firstly tell you a little bit about me, then tell you a little bit about us, the organisation I represent and hopefully you will tell me about yourself and your organisation.' Nick, this is the simplest start to any sales meeting structure that I know. All you have to do is think about creating a position statement, a brief statement about you and the company before asking the prospective client about themselves. Nick when you are putting the positioning statement together, ask yourself, 'so what?' about each statement. 'We have a triple A rating.' So what? 'Mr Client we have a triple A rating, the reason why this is important is we believe that when choosing a financial partner the stability of the company will be a key consideration'."

I took that onboard in the short pause before Pele continued.

"Nick at the beginning of the meeting you lost track slightly and found yourself talking about my nice office and generally making small talk, why?"

"I was taught that it is important to break the ice!"

"Breaking the ice is generally a weak start to a sales call, it is an attempt to try and build rapport by trying to show some level of interest in the person and their surroundings which generally comes over as insincere."

"That goes against what I have been told."

"Well Nick, there is a difference between breaking the ice and finding common ground. The higher up the corporate ladder you go and the more important the prospect is, the less opportunity you have for small talk. Besides, you broke the ice when you made the appointment. Nick, do you really believe, other than through politeness, anyone cares whether you like the view out of my window?"

"Well no, I suppose not."

"See Nick, common ground is different because it builds on the mutual reason for meeting. So when you called and said, 'I have a service that helps people accumulate wealth', that is the common ground. So even if I was to do 'nice view', breaking the ice and being polite, I will need to get to the objective really quickly by referring to the reason for meeting."

I said nothing, waiting for Pele to continue. What he had just said made complete sense and made me feel like a schoolboy in some respects, but I was only repeating what I had been taught to say. Pele gave me a moment to reflect on this then continued.

" 'Mr X, thankyou for taking time out of your schedule and for seeing me today. As I said on the phone I would take only 10 minutes of your time to talk about wealth accumulation'. Nick it is always important to remember that the process is sequential. What happens at one part sets the context for the other part."

"I am not following you, Pele."

"Okay Nick, you said on the phone you were going to meet to talk about wealth accumulation and you would take ten minutes right?"

"Yes that is right."

"So the context is set, that the reason for the meeting is to talk about wealth accumulation and it will take ten minutes. What is the prospect thinking you are coming for and for how long?"

"Ten minutes and wealth accumulation."

"Correct, that is why the content must follow the context. See Nick, Context and Content equals Meaning so you have to make reference to both for continuity of the process. Write that down."

Context And Content Equals Meaning

I had already grabbed the pen and my notebook. "Okay, I understand that now and it makes sense, but how do I get from ten minutes to an hour, which is what I really need?"

"Certainly not from where you are within this meeting. So Nick, let's get back to the main objective of this meeting, Wealth accumulation. You need to create enough interest in what you do to make the client agree to extend the meeting."

"Sorry Pele, I don't have a clue how I would do that."

"That's Okay Nick. Bearing in mind what I said about context and content equalling meaning, we have to create a context for wealth accumulation for the prospect."

I sat there listening intently, trying to take all of this in. This was a new approach for me and even though I was following what Pele was saying, I really didn't have a clue how I would do it.

"So any thoughts what you would do, or say Nick?"

I was going to make a half hearted attempt to look competent but decided against it. "Well Pele, I don't actually know what I would do." The truth of it was, I was so stuck in my habitual thinking I was unable to see any alternatives.

"Nick, let's do this. I will be the sales guy and you be the prospect."

"Yes sure." This will be good, a thought went through my mind about being the most difficult prospect I could be.

"Nick, so we have done the introduction, the ME US YOU, now taking control of the meeting I need to create the context. So Nick, wealth accumulation is a large topic, however, what I find from talking to clients every day is this," he took a piece of paper and put a line straight across the top with 1 at one end and 80 at the other. "Most people live to around 80, so what I have found is that wealth accumulation can be broken down into four key areas."

He drew a circle and cut the circle into four segments. In the first segment he wrote 'education' and '1-20' and said, "one of our largest expenses is our children and their education. Hopefully we give them a good education and we have had a good education, ourselves".

He then wrote '20-40 asset building'. "Then after our education we get a job and start on our career where we are working and earning money and trying to build assets. At this stage Nick we are generally income dependant, do you agree?"

"Yes, I do."

Then he wrote '40-60 Assets consolidation'. "Then Nick, we move to an asset accumulation stage where we are entering our best earning years and are starting to consolidate assets and think about our retirement."

Then he wrote '60-80' and said, "Then we hopefully enter retirement with enough assets to allow us to retire and live out our lives in the way we choose with financial freedom. Nick, which area would you say is most important for you?"

I pointed to the building assets segment. Pele then said, "As I said, I would only take ten minutes of your time today and we are close to that now. Do I have your permission to continue or shall we make a meeting for another day?"

Without thinking I said, "no, please carry on." So much for being a tough prospect! He had completely disarmed me.

"See Nick, how important it is to build a context for what you are going to say and do it in a way that the client is interested?"

"Yes I can see that. What happens if they say 'let's set another meeting'?"

"Then that is fine, just set another meeting. What I have found is if a prospective client says I would like to set up a meeting, he/she is serious about working with me."

"What do I do next though, Pele?"

"Good question, Nick. Before we get to the next stage you need to practice the first 10 minutes."

Pele got me to write a short paragraph about me, a short paragraph about the company then use them in the role play. He had me practice building the context using my own words and after a couple of hours I had it going reasonable well.

"That is good Nick. Now we have the structure for the first 10 minutes flowing well, we have more chance of building a key element of the sales meeting. Credibility."

"See Nick, there are three key elements of a sales meeting. Credibility, Trust and Rapport."

Credibility Trust Rapport

"So Nick, how do you establish Credibility?"

"Well, I would say, coming over as professional."

"Ok so give me an example?"

"Well knowing the sales structure."

"Good, you need to demonstrate expertise. You need to be up to date on the industry you are in, you need to understand your products and your company. You need to demonstrate you know what you are doing in front of the client. That is why structure is important. Fumbling around creates the impression you don't know what you are doing."

"How about what you look like, Pele?"

"Yes certainly Nick, a client's perception is impacted if you don't fit in with what they were expecting. Clearly there are cultural variations on what is acceptable however you should know these as part of your building credibility. Trust, Nick, how do you demonstrate it?"

"I am not sure Pele, is it not just an outcome from a relationship over time?"

"Well Nick, I understand what you are saying, however firstly you must do what you say you will do as a starting point. Remember, trust is always easier to lose than it is to gain. As to over time as you suggest Nick, it is ultimately irrelevant as once you lose someone's trust it is very difficult to ever get it back. The biggest part of trust is being truthful, not always easy if you are focused on the sale only. Sometimes truth is seen as a relative thing to be bent a little to suit ourselves. It is a misconception, Nick, to believe selling is about manipulating the truth or the client. The best way is to establish a trust criteria for yourself. Something that you are happy to constantly demonstrate."

I was starting to get overwhelmed mentally, selling was getting more difficult than I thought. I was thinking I would scrap everything I had ever learned. The simile was that of going to the golf pro for a few tweaks in your game and them taking you right back to basics, even down to the way you hold the club.

I wrote a few trust criteria down and all I could think is whether I could always demonstrate them. It called for me again to have to change my approach to life, not just selling.

1. Am I demonstrating integrity?
2. Am I being reliable?
3. Am I doing what I said I would do?
4. Do I stick to my commitments?
5. Am I telling the truth rather than bending the truth to suit myself?

"Nick, build your list of clients and stick to them. Trust will come from the way you demonstrate these five questions to the clients, especially when you are dealing with clients' money. Let's take a comfort break and grab a cup of tea or a drink."

Relief! I thought my brain was hurting from all this thinking. I got up and walked towards the door, leaving all my stuff on the conference table. Pele followed behind me. I turned right toward the bathroom he turned left towards his office. I walked into the

Gent's and was glad it was empty. Whilst washing my hands I stared into the mirror. 'Come on Nick, you can do this' I said to myself, looking for internal inspiration. I had been given a shed load by Pele throughout the day. I so wanted to get it right to show him I was worth his investing his time in me. I left the Gent's and headed back to the conference room, Pele was already back with cups of tea for us.

"I thought you might want a cup of tea, white one sugar, if I remember correctly?"

"Yes that's great Pele, thank you." I sat down, put the cup on the coaster. We just sat there drinking our tea in silence, it was a real peaceful silence, not an awkward silence, just a feeling you get when you know that nothing has to be said. We both stared out of the window. I don't know what he was thinking but, it was that feeling of a perfect moment.

When I had finished Pele said, "so where do you go next in the process Nick?"

"I assume I would now ask some questions about his needs?"

"Good, so let's see how you do that."

"Do you want me to role play?"

"Well practice makes perfect Nick."

That perfect feeling of peace and contentment disappeared as quick as the word role play had rolled of his lips.

"Let me set the scene; we are now in the transition stage to the third part of the sales process, the **Dialogue** phase. We will assume you have built the context and have permission to move to the next step. Okay, Nick off you go."

"Thanks Pele. Now you said you were interested in building assets. What are you doing in building assets so far?"

"Well Nick, I have a savings plan."

"Who with?"

"XYZ company."

"Do you think what you are saving is enough?"

"No."

"How much do you want to save?"

"Okay Nick, let's stop for a second. This is not really working even though you have pushed me into the savings box. You could argue that is driving for the sale but it's not the most effective way of doing it. Let's look at language first and what you can do with it. You have been on sales courses before, right?"

"Yes, lots of times."

"Good, then you understand the types of questions. right Nick?"

"Yes I do."

"So give me an example of an open question?"

"Why would you want a savings plan?"

Okay, good. And a closed question?"

"Do you want to buy a savings plan?"

"Excellent Nick. Let me now talk about a concept I use for questioning, elevators of language, write that down."

Elevators Of Language

"Nick, gaining customer commitment and gaining understanding come from using language in a certain way and firing off questions in rapid succession and mostly closed will feel like being in a police interrogation. You need to ask the question and let the person think about it first before asking the next one, without driving them straight to the pot of gold."

He paused and gave me time to think this over, then continued. "So your questions were fine Nick, however you really didn't gain an understanding and once I said savings plan your whole questioning focused on this. Your questions became closed questions and pushed me straight into the down elevator. I will explain the elevators in a moment before we look at the types of questions such as, probing questions, open versus closed questions and so on. Let's discuss the elevators. Elevators, as the name suggests, raise the conversation from level to level. They take the conversation up and down dependant on what I want from the client or prospect. If you want to move someone around in a conversation you can do that by moving them into either the up or down elevator. If you try and move across elevators this is not possible without disagreement. Agreement, Nick, is often found in ambiguity, whereas disagreement is easier found in detail. An example is; lets imagine we were having a conversation about cars and I wanted to talk about buses. I could go straight across the elevators and say, 'I hear what you say about cars but I want to talk about buses.' Not the best sales approach is it? If I want to talk about cars, it would be easy. I could move the client straight into a discussion by asking a 'what specifically', a down elevator question. That's the kind of question that drives them straight into a detailed answer."

I said nothing, just sat there soaking it all up.

"Down elevator questions are; 'what specifically do you like about cars?' or 'what specific car would you buy, if money was not a consideration'. However Nick, lets say I want to talk about buses, then I need the up elevator. 'So Nick, cars are fascinating I agree. In reality, what is the main purpose of a car?' Purpose puts them into the Up Elevator and a move towards ambiguity. What would you say Nick?"

"Well I suppose transport or movement."

"That's interesting, Nick. So what other forms of transport are available other than a car?"

"Well, I suppose trains, planes, buses, roller blades, bikes."

"Interesting you mention buses Nick. Let's chat about the benefits of using a bus rather than a car. What would be the benefits of using a bus"?

"I don't know, perhaps no issues with parking, cheaper to run, I could network on a bus."

"This is, of course, a simplified example, Nick and it doesn't pretend to be the level of dialogue you would engage in with your prospects. However it does demonstrate the concept of how to focus on moving the client up and down and just using the type of question to do that. You never openly disagree with the prospect, you simply steer the conversation into the right elevator and allow the prospect to push the buttons for the floor you want them to go to. Naturally, making it happen in real life, real time, with real prospects takes practice but it doesn't have to be difficult, either. Once you grasp the concept of steering the conversation, the Elevators of Language, you can very quickly improve your performance. Now, write down open and closed questions."

Open And Closed Questions

"Nick, unless you understand the dynamics of language and use the Elevators of Language then leaning to ask an open question or a closed question is as helpful as a chocolate ashtray. Even though you demonstrated you knew what an open or closed question was we still ended up very quickly in the down elevator going to the basement. You are not the only person to do this, most people do the same. They forget about understanding the customer and get straight back to questioning as being the tool to make sales. Questioning is a tool for understanding and sales are an outcome from that understanding Nick."

I realised I was almost off the edge of my chair. I had been paying such close attention I had unknowingly moved closer and closer to him. I sat back and tried to relax and just open my mind to take in everything he was saying.

"We should also talk about the questioning funnel, Nick, as a generic structure that works for keeping your questioning on track. All these tools will be helpful in your sales meetings, give them structure and allow them to flow smoothly. Have you come across the funnel technique Nick?"

"Yes, but I do get slightly confused between the funnel in sales and the funnel in questioning?"

"Well, in simple terms they are both a way in which you remember certain parts of a process. The sales funnel demonstrates the overall sales process; a top down look at it, from gaining leads through to servicing the clients. The questioning funnel is more specific and looks at which question to use where, however this is easier to draw on a sheet paper than, it is to actually do. So tell me Nick what do you remember about the funnel?"

Pele drew a funnel on a piece of paper and pushed it over to me. I was confident I knew what to write and wrote open questions, probing questions, and closed questions evenly spaced going down the funnel. I was feeling smug as Pele looked down at the paper. I should have remembered the old saying about pride before a fall.

"This is good Nick, yet it isn't the complete funnel."

I felt gutted, I was sure that was what the trainer had taught us.

"Nick, a question for you. You can look in your notes if you want. What was the thing I said to you about selling other than it is an art or a science?"

I thumbed through the pages quickly, thinking I hoped I'd written it down. Back in 'Discovery' part of my notes I had written was; *'Selling is and Art and a Science and you have to gain the prospects commitment to the next step in the process'*. I said, "I have written 'gain commitment from the prospect'."

"That is correct Nick. So how do you do that, with the first question being open in the funnel?"

"I don't know Pele, I remember being taught that you ask an open question first."

"Actually Nick, the first question is a closed question, it is to gain commitment to ask questions."

"I don't understand Pele?"

"Nick, it is very simple to remember. For me to understand how much you know about the funnel Nick, do you mind if I ask you a few questions?"

"Yes sure." I didn't realise he had just demonstrated it, I was expecting something else.

"There you go Nick, easy isn't it? Permission to ask a question but you always loop back to the same question to restart the funnel."

"Can you give me a demonstration as I am still struggling with it.?"

"Sure. The loop back works like this. Let's say the prospect or client, Mrs Y, says something like; 'I don't think you really understand what I am trying to achieve.' You can say; 'Okay Mrs Y, for me to really understand what you are trying to achieve can I ask you some more questions?', understand?"

"Yes, I get this Pele."

"So what do you do now given her statement?"

"I ask an open question as per the funnel."

"See Nick, a couple of things to consider. Firstly it would depend on where you were in the overall process to which question you ask her. Secondly the funnel appears to be a one way process and is normally demonstrated as such. It is not. It is a fluid process and should really be demonstrated with the arrows going up and down a bit like my elevators. The reason why I say this is because dependant on where you are in the process I might need to go into the down elevator straight away. Which is not an open question is it?"

"No, a closed one."

"So in the **DECISION** part of the sales process, which we will talk about later, let's imagine I have been presenting to Mrs Y and this could be resistance from the client. I might then want to say something like; 'Mrs Y, you say I don't understand what you are trying to achieve, what specifically have I missed that would make you believe that?' I have to say in reality Nick, if I was presenting and this came up as an objection or what I prefer to call client resistance, I would be disappointed in my earlier failure to understand the client. Let's go to an earlier stage of the sales process. Say this comes out in the **DIRECTION** part of the process, then the up elevator might be the most appropriate way to go and then the open question could be something like; 'as it is really important that I understand what you are trying to achieve, do you mind if I ask you a few questions?' That's the top of the funnel. One open question is; 'how can I change my understanding and help you achieve what you want?' See how I did that Nick? Top of the funnel and then the open question. The other way to think about the start of the funnel is 'WIIFM'."

"What is that?"

"WIIFM, 'What's in it for me' is a principle that makes you again change your perceptual position to that of the client. In questioning it helps you to structure the question in a way that highlights the benefits to the client. 'For me to really understand your requirements do you mind if I ask you a few questions'. 'For us both to get the most out of this meeting, Nick, do you mind if I ask you a few questions?' See how that works?"

"Yes that's good, I get that." I wrote it down.

WIIFM. What's In It For Me?

"Nick you also need to remember this is a conversation about people and their thoughts, the things that matter to them. It certainly isn't about rushing through a process to get to a sale. There isn't simply a set number of questions you can ask. Just go with the flow and listen to them and care enough that you get it right."

I sat there thinking. Pele's demonstration off the top of his head was slick, it was just like water off a ducks back to him. He was in his element training and coaching me, I could see the passion in every thing he said and did. It really was a blessing, having had such a rubbish year, to actually get to sit with him to go through this stuff.

"Nick, what I need us to do now is practice going through the actual funnel process."

"Great Pele, that works for me."

So I wrote down the list in my notepad as Pele said them:

1 Closed question (gain permission to ask the series of questions - WIIFM)

2 Prime open questions (open question used to get information to give better understanding)

3 Probing question (open question that builds on prime question and delves into any ambiguities and probes deeper)

4 Closed questions (seek specific pieces of information)

"Nick there are a few things that we should add to the structure, so write this down. At the end of the funnel you will start to gather information that will separate into two funnels. One is general understanding and the other will be the client's or prospect's buying requirements. These requirements will be funnels in their own right, so you need to work each client's requirements through the same process so you completely understand it."

"Do you have an example Pele?"

"Of course Nick, so when you sit with the prospects that you have just made the meetings with you will go into the **DIRECTION** part of the sales process. You will control the meeting through the structure you have learned. You will get the client to genuinely want to extend the meeting with you and then you will use the questioning techniques we are talking about here. You will then gain both general and specific information about the prospect and specific wealth accumulation information that relates to the prospect. So conceptually, you will have a big funnel for the client, then you will create specific individual funnels for his specific individual requirements. So imagine Nick, the client will say he has three children. This goes into the general funnel to start the questioning. You identify he wants to send them to boarding school and requires school fees planning. You then create a funnel called 'schools fees planning'. However, you also discover that he is 45 and wants to retire at 60 and has an underlying requirement to fund for his retirement. You create another funnel called 'retirement.' Now by doing this the big funnel is generic and is the **DIRECTION** stage of the sales process. As you move to individual funnels you move into what I call the **DIALOGUE** stage of the process which I will talk about later. Either way Nick, the funnel allows you to structure the meeting and ensure you capture all the relevant requirements. Do you understand Nick?"

"Yes Pele, I do and it's great. In fact I was thinking it seems so simple it is scary. Can it really be this easy?"

"At the end of each funnel is what I call the summary question. It basically checks each funnel is complete. You say something like this; 'is there anything with regards your children's education or school fees planning that I have missed?' Or, 'is there anything I have not asked about your retirement planning that you think is important?' This makes sure that you completely understand each funnel, Nick."

This has really kickstarted my internal motivation to want to go out and try it. I had a strange feeling building, it actually was the feeling of enthusiasm, a feeling that had been eluding me for the whole year.

"So Nick, how do you feel about the questioning part of the process?"

"It is really good and you make it seem simple."

"It is simple. It is your application of it that will determine whether it is simple for you. We should practice this now Nick, before moving on to the next section of the process."

We spent the next couple of hours practicing each funnel and as I looked out of the window, I could see the sun going down on the day. It cast its glow across the walls of glass in the buildings that made up the city, reflecting it straight into the conference room as it cut across the table and shone it's orange light on the white wall. A perfect end to a perfect day I thought.

Pele said, "let's call it a day Nick and I will see you tomorrow bright and early so we can go through the DIALOGUE section before we start on the prospect meeting."

"Sure Pele, what time shall we meet?"

"Well let's say 7:30 for coffee and an 8 am start, does that work for you?"

"Yes, no problem." I was actually thinking I haven't been up before 8 in a while let alone a 7:30 start. I was, however, still feeling excited about going out to practice the things I had learned. Pele and I walked to the elevators as half the office seemed to be emptying out for the lifts. The lift doors opened as I arrived and I seemed to get drawn in by the crowd. I didn't really a get chance to say thank you to him. I turned to see the doors closing and Pele smiling at me between the closing doors. I found myself thinking that like life itself, it is so easy to get dragged along with the crowd and not say and do the things that are important.

Chapter 3 Dialogue

'Everything begins with Dialogue, Dialogue is the initial
step in creation of value, Dialogue is the starting point and
underlying force in all human relationships'
Daisaku Ikeda

The following morning I was up early, even before my PDA
had lit up the room with its fluorescent glow. My mind had wok-
en me around 4:30, racing through the things I had to do.
Trepidation about the day before me was foremost in my mind.
I would have to remember everything I had learned yesterday,
plus all the information I would get today before my meetings
with Pele would fall into line and begin to make real sense.

I was on my way early, in fact so early that at this time of the
morning, the traffic was surprisingly light. As I looked out of the
window of the cab the sky was clear and it was going to be another nice day. I put the window down and took in the air as it
blew across my face. I couldn't help thinking that my decision to
go into the office around 6:30-7:00 am would be a waste of time
but it was nothing other than my addiction to my bed and a dash
of self-doubt. It was in fact quieter than at 8:30 plus, I had plenty
of time to reflect and get my thoughts together for the day
ahead.

I arrived at head office early, in fact early enough to sit in the
coffee shop on the ground floor. I watched people on their way
to work and wondered what they all did for a living. That trig-
gered the next thought, of how many of these people could be
clients or prospects. Pele was right, it is really interesting, the di-
versity of people who you can meet in sales.

I looked at my watch; 7:14. Time to get upstairs, don't want to be late. I finished the tea and threw the take away cup in the bin on my way back into the foyer. The elevator was already on 'Ground', so as I pushed the button, the door opened immediately. I entered the lift and as it was empty I went straight to the management floor. I got out to an empty reception area, so I walked around to Pele's office. I could smell the aroma of coffee as I got closer. I thought Pele must be in already. His door was open so I put my head round the door and saw he was sat on the couch with his eyes closed.

"Hi Pele." Nothing, he just sat there, still as a post with his eyes closed. I stood waiting for a response; still nothing for at least 5 minutes that felt like hours.

He then opened his eyes and said, "Good morning Nick. I see you are early today which is a good sign. My assumption rests on your motivation I hope rather than your inability to sleep."

"Yes Pele, I am keen as mustard." I don't even know whether he understood what that meant, but hey. "I didn't want to disturb you" I said.

"You didn't disturb me Nick, I was meditating, which I do every day. 30 minutes in the morning and 30 minutes at night; it helps me consolidate all my learning. The morning sets me up for how I want the day to go and in the evening I consolidate my learning."

"Does that actually work Pele? I always thought it was all in the mind."

"Well Nick, firstly it does the opposite; it gets you out of your brain and all that noise that you create and into your mind. Secondly it does work for me and I would recommend it. The challenge for you, of course Nick, is as you identified yesterday; it would call for change in your routine, your habitual thinking. I believe it is incorrect that you think brain and mind are the same thing; the brain is the access tool for the mind and the mind and what we call consciousness. Consciousness doesn't only include your consciousness because, we are all part of the greater system Nick it incorporates group consciousness. It is this energy that flows between us and makes us part of the same system. It is your brain that pulls memories and thoughts into your consciousness when you think"

That was true but I wanted to question that statement. "When you said, 'out of your brain and into your Mind', what did that mean?" It was back to a series of the 'X Files' and too deep a topic for 7:23 am!

"That is for another day and another coaching session, however, it is fair to say that the brain and the mind are not the same thing. It is incorrect that you think they are the same. The brain is the access tool for the mind and it is consciousness that the brain pulls your memories and thoughts into when you think. We can talk about the conscious mind in dialogue later. Right Nick, the coffee is ready so let's get going."

Great. But I was now intrigued, my brain was working over time trying to process what had just been said. If this is the depth of the conversation at 7:24 it's going to be a deeply reflective day.

Pele poured the coffee and I sat on the couch as I did yesterday. This time instead of trepidation and fear, my emotive state was one of excitement and anticipation.

"Okay Nick" Pele began as he put my coffee down. "Where is your notepad and more importantly my Pen?"

I had found it in my pocket when I got home, I almost stuck it to my forehead so I wouldn't forget it. "Here it is."

"Good, then write 'dialogue'."

Dialogue

"Just before I recap on yesterday Nick, I want you to close your eyes."

I thought, 'what is this, a meditation session?' I did as instructed as I was interested in where it would go.

"Okay Nick, I want you to close your eyes and stare into the back of your eyelids. Imagine looking up just under the bottom of the eye socket, can you do that now?"

I shut my eyes and tried to look into the back of my eye lids, looking up just under the eye sockets as instructed. It was hard;

my eyes kept coming down to stare centrally in the eye. I opened my eyes and said, "it's hard keeping my eyes up there Pele."

"I know Nick, you have to preserve, it requires discipline. This time try again and focus on keeping them there and count backwards from one hundred to zero. Do that now."

So I started inwardly focusing, keeping my eyes staring upwards whilst counting backwards. When I got to about fifty I had no thoughts, for a split second I seemed to slip between all my thoughts. As soon as I recognised I was in that nothingness between thought, I lost it. The thoughts rushed back in. I was disappointed but I reset my eyes and started counting again, trying to regain that mental state.

I could hear Pele slowing his pace of speech down and, saying softly in the background; "When you get to zero, Nick, hold that mental state and imagine mentally running over all the things you learned yesterday. That's right, the DIRECTION section of the process, you are focusing now on picking out your key learnings. Now as you do that, imagine writing them in your note pad in your mind now. That's it Nick. Now grab your index finger. Keep seeing the key points entering your pages in your mind. Now, in your mind's eye as you right them down they should line up under the heading of DIRECTION. You have a realisation, that whenever you need to recap on them you can mentally do that anytime now. And as I count backward from three to one as you open your eyes you will know the learning is always there and you will feel refreshed, 3-2-1"

When I opened my eyes I did feel refreshed and I could see in my mind the notepad with 'Direction' and all the points I had written down.

"Let's get going Nick, we have a lot to do today."

I didn't say anything but I thought we had been going ages already.

"So as part of your sales process you should always learn to recap from the last time you talked with the prospect or client. See mentally for me, Nick, I presuppose that all the meetings are just extensions of the same meeting. Instead of considering time as past, present and future I just presuppose I am in the present. It is almost like we have just been in a coffee or tea break, Nick."

I sat and thought about that for a second and even though at one level it was deep, at a practical level it made complete sense to me. "That's a really unique way of thinking about it Pele."

"Good Nick, then let's do a quick recap on the funnels and questioning before we look at communication and the dialogue process in more detail. Remember what we said about creating the big funnel as the generic client/prospect funnel? This is really in the 'DIRECTION' stage of the sales process where you are mainly controlling the meeting. You are establishing credibility and trust with the client through a nice easy flowing rhythm to your first 10 minutes. Then the client allows you to move to the second part of the sales process, what I call the 'DIALOGUE' process where you create individual funnels for each of the client or Prospects requirements. Then Nick I concluded by talking about the summary question which checked each funnel is complete. Is that a fair summary of where we left off?"

"Yes, perfect."

"Good, what I am going to do now, Nick, is give you a high level, or big picture, view of communication and then move you down into the detail of each piece of it and how it works in the sales process. Does that work for you, Nick?"

"Yes perfect." I suddenly realise he is gaining commitment from me to each step as we go, it is almost like the process in action, even as he is coaching me.

"Nick, what is the meaning of communication?"

I quickly thumbed through my notes. I had heard that before. "The response that you get."

"Well done Nick and part of that meaning comes from the context and the content that you use with the client. Nick give me one word that describes Love?"

I thought for a second. "Passion."

"Okay and one that describes humour?"

"I suppose 'funny'."

Pele picked up the handset and called Claire from reception. She came in quickly and said, "morning Pele."

Pele stood up and said, "morning Claire" as she entered the room. I looked at him and realised what had just happened, but it was too late for me to get up, I was just the young, rude git slouching on the couch. "Thankyou for coming to our rescue. Can you give me one word that describes Love?"

She stood there looking at me, probably thinking; 'why are you wasting your time on him, Pele?'

She said, "beauty."

"Thankyou Claire. And just one more, one word for 'Humour'?"

"Comedian."

"Perfect, thanks for helping us."

She said, "my pleasure" and walked out of the office.

"See Nick, two universal words that everyone would know. If I asked half the office in here we would get a whole host of different answers. The thing is that by actually generating different words it probably means the underlining meaning is different. This means the experience of love may create a different definition of it for different people. Now the financial services world is full of jargon, as are many industries, however we must as sales people remember, most of our clients don't understand any of it. Even if they appear to at first sight, their understanding and what we mean maybe different."

I sat and wrote 'love' and 'humour' in my book and contemplated how often I rattled away in financial jargon to prospects and clients. This was something I had never really given any thought to.

"So, even though the meaning of communication is the response you get, part of that will come from both the context the word is used in and the word itself. Which brings us to the non verbal piece of communication."

Pele leaned over the table and pointed his finger right in my face and said, "I really like you in a really aggressive way. See, Nick, the words themselves can be deceiving but throw in the context of gestures and tonality and it could change the entire meaning."

I was just sat there taking notes finding what Pele had to say as being really interesting stuff. I was hoping the day would continue in this vain, as Pele was doing all the work and I was enjoying just listening.

"It is surprising that when you know someone quite well you can pick up changes in tone, gestures, etcetera that are not obvious to anyone else. An example of that Nick is, well have you ever been lying down on your bed or perhaps the sofa and your mobile rings. You pick it up and it is your Mother, or someone close to you and you start talking and with a few seconds they say, 'hey Nick are you lying down?'."

"Yes loads of times but I had not thought of it."

"How do they know other than through the subtle change in your tonality. We are all masters of this, however most of the time we are so wrapped up in what we are saying we forget the more subtle pieces of communication that are coming from the prospect or client. Also some prospects use non verbal cues as any easy option to answering your poorly worded questions. An example maybe, to fold their arms and lean away from you, whilst still agreeing with a single worded yes. This could mean yes, or this could mean, 'I don't entirely agree hence my moving away but it is easier to just say yes to this sales bloke'. Ok Nick, let me ask you a question. How important is eye contact?"

"It is a must, Pele, we should always maintain eye contact."

"Correct Nick. But remember all this is given a certain context. Staring too long at a group of guys on a street corner with their hoodies on, in certain parts of the city, well it might be ill advised. Write this down in you note pad Nick, then we will talk about it."

Rapport And Congruence

"Pele how do you spell 'congruence'? Pele spelt out CONGRUENCE for me as I wrote it down.

"Nick it is important to realise, I have a different view than most about 'Rapport', as I said earlier I presuppose it is constant. Most people including most books on the subject believe the techniques you use create it and therefore would disagree with what I am telling you. You must make your own mind up Nick as you are your own man. I want you to think of it in the context I will give you now. For me it is fundamental to understanding why the techniques of matching and mirroring etcetera work."

Okay great, I thought, some controversy so early in the day.

"Nick, have you ever been stood in a room and had the sixth sense or deep perception that someone is staring at you? Have you ever stood in a bar staring at someone and they look over straight at you?"

"Sure, Pele, loads of times."

"So what is that? What is happening?"

"I suppose it is instinct?"

"Instinct deals with behaviour Nick, this is more of an intuition or perception outside of your normal senses. It is a way of looking at a cause and effect relationship outside of our logical thinking."

"I am trying to link this to body language, Pele, and how it fits and I am getting lost a bit."

"As I said before Nick, you were lost and now you were found. Okay Nick, imagine lying in a bath and the water is just up to your nose, so you are looking down at a bath of still water; can you imagine that?"

"Sure I do it all the time."

"Good, so as you are lying there, you take your hand and softly tap the surface of the water; what happens?"

"A wave moves away from me down the bath."

"What happens when it hits the bath?"

"It comes back to me."

"So, Nick, imagine now that you're in the bar and you feel someone staring at you and instead of not knowing what is going on you realise 'I am feeling the energy coming from that person over there staring at me'. That's the sudden realisation, that all your thoughts are pure energy and when you send them out into the ether, they have intention."

This was an amazing way at looking at something. I was lost for words, I just sat waiting for him to continue. I had no possible response to this presupposition as it just felt intuitive and true.

"Nick, right back at the start of our chat yesterday we talked about us all being one part of a big system; this is the connection to body language."

I sat there saying nothing, waiting, knowing now, that over my short interaction of two days with Pele, his thinking was so much deeper than mine. I was only thinking sales, he was putting life into sales by linking complex thinking into simple terms for me to understand. I had to admit, it all made sense to me as I sat there waiting for its profound application to come. It wasn't long coming, about 5 seconds to be exact, as he looked straight into my eyes.

"Do you know Nick, body language is all about pooling energy?"

"No Pele, I don't." It was probably a rhetorical question but I answered anyway.

"Let's explore some examples in your every day life Nick. When you go into a sales meeting or meet someone for the first time, do you ever notice their body positions when they communicate with you?"

"Actually Pele, with body language, I was taught all the stuff about 93% of communication is non verbal and 7 % is the words. That's all I can remember, I really don't look at body positions. I'm normally concentrating on the 7% of what they say so I don't mess it up."

"Well that's truthful Nick, we can chat about Dr Albert Mehrabian's research if you want, however as most of his research was miss quoted, just stick with the fact body language is much larger than the words themselves."

"Okay, cool."

"So, body positions Nick. What do you notice with clients, or just people?"

I sat there for a second or two recollecting the start of some of my sales meetings. "Yes, Pele, I can think of how people generally react when they meet me for the first time in a sales situation."

"Good, what happens?"

"Well, generally what happens is I sit down and they sit down. Normally then they lean back in their chairs or cross their arms."

"Okay, what is happening when they do this?"

"I was told they are uneasy with me because I am in sales."

"Right. Nick, let's examine this; firstly write this in your book under 'DIALOGUE'. It would be obvious and easy to make the assumption that they are uneasy with you because you are in sales. This thinking is classic yet it is actually superficial with regards to people and communication. The presupposition here is that 'Rapport' is constant due to the energy being constant but neutral. From the evidence you would think, no way, because I am not experiencing this given this situation."

No kidding Sherlock! I was thinking that and also.

"Actually Nick, what the client is doing is pooling his or her energy."

I wrote in my notepad:

Pooling Energy And Body Language

"If you think about the bath and the way we send thoughts out with intention, as the perceiver we are completely instinctive about its movement. This is not a conscious thing we do, we do it instinctively. Body language tools and techniques that are normally taught attempt to make this a conscious process, which is fine, we can talk about that later. However the client or prospect in a sales context is pooling energy. Why then?"

Before I could answer 'yes why?' he continued.

"Because at an intuitive level, beyond your conscious mind, we have learned to protect ourselves this way. So in an attempt to stop him or herself getting close to you because you are a sales person they must pool energy. The person will want to control the flow of energy or in this context, Rapport, by stopping the flow between you. The outcome of this is the folding of the arms the creating of space between them and you and all the other ways in which people pool their energy. It is a instinctive protection against letting their true feelings be revealed. The client will create a so called '**CLOSED POSITION**'. Now the statement, 'Rapport is constant', can be thought of as the energy between you is constant until you **MAKE WAVES** Nick. Until you make waves and add your intention that energy is neutral or rapport is neutral. As they say Nick, '**don't make waves**'. Until you have the **intention** and splash the hand on the water in the bath, no wave happens. Until you think Nick, energy is like the bath water. It is just being energy. It is you pulling energy into your consciousness by creating a thought that starts the process. As soon as that thought is formulated energy is sent out into the ether."

He gave me a moment to reflect on this, then carried on.

"Now let's think of the client or prospect. He or she is creating thoughts all the time, as you are, and as these build up into a series of thoughts which create a pool of energy which we call perception. It is this pool of energy that we feel and we say I instinctively knew he or she was thinking that. It is your thinking and the intentions of those thoughts that mould the energy that creates feelings. It is this energy we call 'Rapport'. We say things like, 'I just knew I had a good feeling when I was with her or him'. 'I was comfortable when I was around them'. 'I had a good feeling when he was talking to me'. Splashing around in your thoughts every day, not knowing what you are creating, Nick, is for amateurs or worse, people that believe they are victims of life and circumstances. Mastery comes from realising that we are all interconnected and our thoughts have our **intentions** manifest and have a direct impact on the whole system."

This was deep, but it made perfect sense. I could recall situations and meetings where what he just said finally made sense of what had happened in them.

"If we are not careful, Nick, we allow ourselves, through our ego, our beliefs, to say that there is no connection between anything or anyone. That we are individuals and completely separated in every way. This leads to all our problems in life and, in this context, sales. We become self centered for the wrong reasons, it creates an 'I win, you lose' type of thinking. This thinking always ends badly at all levels."

For some reason, I had this overwhelming thought about government policies and religious gtoups but thought I would leave that for another day.

"Nick, remember an important lesson. We all want to be connected. People instinctively know this and the beauty of life is, when we are at one with someone or something else, it is in this moment we find mastery of ourselves. What are you thinking now, Nick?"

"Well, I would know he or she was unhappy about something."

"Exactly, what would you do about it?"

"I don't know Pele."

"Well Nick, what is the point in understanding body language if you then don't do anything about it?"

I sat there thinking about it and he was right. Instinctively, I would sense it in a meeting and then do nothing about it. "What would you suggest Pele?"

"Well, it is about understanding, so you need to understand the change in body language or the client will stack up reasons why they shouldn't buy the product. This will become resistance later, when you present the solution or product. Therefore perhaps a question such as; 'Mr or Mrs Y, I couldn't help but notice or sense, that you feel differently about what I just said. Please let me know what you think about it.' It, of course, being the thing you were talking about. What we should do now, Nick, is look at some of the techniques for enhancing our communication."

I thought we had been but just said; "yes Pele, that is perfect."

"Let's talk about **MATCHING AND MIRRORING**. Do you know anything about matching or mirroring Nick?"

"Well, not really, I thought they were the same thing Pele."

"It is when you copy what the other person is doing I think. He folds his arms, you do the same. Nick let's put what you said into a context so we are on the same page."

"Okay, great."

"So what is it Nick?"

Mirroring Is The Natural Synchronisation Of Your Overall Communication With Another's
Matching Is The Natural Synchronisation Of Your Communication With Yourself

I wrote the above quotes from Pele in my notepad.

"Nick, **MIRRORING** is not only the gestures, it can also be through language. Some examples could be you are talking and you and the prospect both start nodding your heads together and saying 'yes' about a certain point you made. This is a natural occurrence in every day conversation. I emphasize it is a natural occurrence because of the way we use energy. At a personal level, think back to a time perhaps when you were watching couples in the bars, when you are out at night. You can identify really quickly whether there is synchronisation between a couple. They are looking into each other's eyes, their proximity is close and they are both in an open position as they drink they drink together. There is complete synchronisation between them and the energy can almost be felt by everyone who is watching them."

He was right, I had seen this lots of times, yet to be truthful I have seen as many couples doing the opposite. Just sat there playing on their smart phones with little or no synchronisation. "Yes Pele I have seen this lots of times" I said.

"Let's consider how we can manipulate this natural synchronisation in a constructive way. The reason I say manipulate, which can have a negative connotation, is because there is a fine line between consciously doing something and a natural occurrence. In other words, as soon as you start thinking about what you are doing and mirroring, you move from natural occurrence to manipulating this situation, irrespective of intention. Mirroring in most books is about the manipulation, however, it is used in a constructive way to increase rapport. It is also positive because we have a positive intention, to speed up the process for a genuine reason of knowing someone better. Anything else won't work Nick, because it is just manipulation and clients will know as we are all one system. Matching is, as I said, when your whole communication is synchronised with you. So when what you think, say and do are all congruent to yourself, you are in harmony. In other words Nick, if you know what you're selling is not right for a client and you say it is, you will not be congruent with the other person and they will recognise it. The other part of matching and mirroring is Pacing and Leading. They are linked and are all ways of enhancing rapport."

Matching and mirroring, pacing and leading, I was confused. Pacing and leading? I couldn't help thinking it sounded like dog training. I am sure it had its application and waited for Pele to explain it to me. I wrote **Pacing and Leading** on my note pad.

"Nick there are two parts to consider when we talk about pacing and leading. Firstly the non verbal pacing and leading and also the verbal pacing and leading. I will talk about the non verbal bit first and we can talk about the actual verbal pacing and leading later, especially when we look at negotiating and influencing people."

I added:

Non Verbal Pacing and Leading
Verbal Pacing and Leading

"Rapport is, as I have said earlier, when you are completely in tune with their energy, Nick. So as I said the client or prospect attempts to control the flow of energy between you and them. An example is when you first meet them they pool their energy by closing off the flow to you. Pacing someone is to recognise what is happening and consciously mirror them. This doesn't mean mimicking them, it is trying to get the other person to realise there is no requirement for them to pool their energy as they have nothing to fear. So what sort of things are practical, Nick?"

I raced to think of a sensible response before realising it had been a rhetorical question. Fortunately Pele continued before I had a chance to embarrass myself and say something just so he didn't think I was missing the point entirely.

"Well, tonality and pace of speech for one, listening to the tone and pace of the prospect or client. If they are talking quietly and delivering the words slowly, say. You might need to slow your delivery and lower your tone in line with theirs. Notice their body position. Are they sat back in their chair? Are they positioned so the energy is flowing away from you? If so, you should do the same; sit back and position yourself so your energy is flowing away also. You need it to be comfortable for you and them and not obvious. What happens then is you test openness and flow (rapport between you) by leading. You may lean forward across the table with your pen and say, 'Mr X, I would like to show you this', pointing at your brochure or diagram. He or she should move forward to meet you. You then keep the space close by not returning to sitting back in the chair. If they stay forward on the table it is a good indication you have created an increase in your rapport and the relationship is moving in the intended direction. The other thing in leading is good eye contact. If it can be maintained without it feeling awkward, that is another good indication of positive energy between you."

"Pele, do we all do this naturally?"

"Nick, as I have said all along, this is all natural. Rapport is a natural occurrence, it is always present in its neutral form. We change it through our thinking and our outward manifestation of our intentions, whether positively or negatively. It is who we are on that day, in that exact moment that people sense themselves. That is why communication, ultimately, is always more than the words themselves."

"Pele I have never heard it explained in that way before, in fact it makes it sound really simple."

"It is really simple, we are the complexity in the process, Nick."

"Let's chat about another important part of communication before we get out and see these prospects."

"How about the verbal pacing and leading Pele?"

"I haven't forgotten Nick, I will do it later, as there are other things we need to cover first."

I was slightly disappointed but I just said, "Okay, great."

"Nick let's just talk about how we all filter our communication. Write down 'communication filters'."

Communication Filters

"Most of the time we are manipulating the language like a child plays with plasticine. One way we manipulate it is by filtering out pieces that maybe less favourable to the client. We also change it in another way, when we filter it out through consciousness into our short term memory."

"What do you mean Pele?"

"It is like having too much material on your hard drive, or in your inbox and it creates an error message, 'please delete to create space'. Well the conscious mind is the same. It holds far too much information for your short term memory, which can only hold a limited amount of information at one time. Have you ever been in a meeting or sales call and you are trying to listen to what the client is saying, while also trying to think of the next question and realise if you don't hold the original thought you'll lose the track of what was being said?"

"I do that all the time, Pele."

"What happens, Nick?"

"I end up missing what they are saying because I am thinking on the words of the question. In fact, Pele, once I have constructed the question in my mind, I am then in a hurry to ask it."

"That's because you are a highly visual type of guy, Nick and as those pictures whizz through your mind you just want to get them out there."

"What do you mean, visual guy?"

"Well Nick, I will cover that later also, however, it means you prefer to use visual mental imagery to process your thinking. In other words Nick, you see a picture in your mind then respond to me or the client using that style. The one thing about using pictures Nick, is you talk faster and in a slightly higher tone. It can mean, and I will generalise here, that you are someone who wants to get it out there quickly as things are just moving too slowly for you."

I listened intently, as he was right, that is exactly what I do. "How do you know that?"

"I would like to deal with the conscious mind and short term memory first, Nick. The reason why it should be in this order is because it will be more beneficial to you and you will learn it quicker and as you know, time and speed is money. I would not want you to have to learn slower and waste your time or money. Is that okay, Nick?"

"Yes, sure, that's fine Pele." I realised he had disarmed me and my need to do that first had gotten kicked into the long grass. He was good at this. I sat there thinking I really hope I can master this stuff as my life could change so much for the better.

"Nick, in 1956 a guy called G. A. Miller wrote a paper called *The Magical Number 7, Plus or Minus 2'* and to put it simply it looked at the short term memory and our ability to recall information. Write down '7 ± 2'. There has been other work carried out since then that ultimately says that instead of plus 7 pieces of information or minus 2 pieces of information, it maybe be as little 3 pieces is all we can hold in our heads, dependant on the chunk size."

"What is a chunk size Pele?"

"A chunk of information is the way we mentally group information so we can recall it. Therefore, your short term memory is like a post-it note in size, it is good to recall or process very small amounts of information and is susceptible to how you do it. The way of increasing that size is, as an example, through grouping the information so you can get more in. Think of it like a zip file. So how does this fit in with sales Nick?"

I was starting to think of the answer but it was rhetorical, as usual, and thankfully he carried on.

"Nick, it is about grouping information in 3 pieces or chunks for the client. The other thing is, for a person to embed the information into long term memory you must have repetition and rehearsal by getting the client to say it more than once. So imagine this sales guy, we'll call him Nick. He goes to see a client and rattles off a whole load of things which he expects the client to remember. The only problem is the client can only recall three things from the meeting. The real problem though is he remembers three wrong things because he didn't know which three to recall."

I started to process this and it not only made sense, I could remember sales calls when this is certainly what must have happened. The client only remembered the problems and not the solutions I had listed so he thought of my services as making things worse and not better! It made sense.

"There was a sales girl who decided that, when she did her meetings, she would structure her language and the process in such a way, that she would identify which three pieces she wanted the client to remember. She ended each section of the process by summarising and repeating the key messages. During her questioning and use of the funnel, she created three key messages for each and reinforced these through reciting them back to the client. She closed the deal as the client recalled why it was such a good idea to take action and buy the product."

As I sat there thinking, it reinforced how important it is not to overload the client with information. I also couldn't help but realise that I needed to reinforce my key messages as three key points for each section of the meeting.

"Which brings us to how we collect the information and build up our key messages around the clients criteria and thoughts. Write this down:"

Know Your Client Financial Needs Analysis

"Nick, as you may be aware, unlike lots of my other clients in different sectors, financial services has a specific regulatory requirement to know your client. This means you must retain the information you collect and link your recommendations to the client data. Now most sales people I work in the field with do this really badly. They struggle to make the transition from the collection of hard and soft facts. In fact I would go as far as saying if they didn't have a compliance and regulatory reason for doing it they wouldn't."

I couldn't help but think, 'no kidding Sherlock'. Most financial services sales guys call compliance the business prevention unit.

Pele looked at me and said, "Even though most of you guys don't like doing it, it is in fact a really useful tool to get the correct information. It also gets the client to agree that what he or she has told you is absolutely correct, especially if you get the 'fact find' signed."

I couldn't help myself, "But Pele, you talked so much about flow and I find this just breaks the flow between me and the client, especially when I am asking questions. To get him or her to sign it in the first meeting is also really difficult."

He smiled and said, "Interesting point, but what is your alternative?"

"What do you mean?"

"Well if you don't do it with the client, you must write the 'fact find' up afterwards and get it signed on your second visit."

Busted! "Well yes, I do this sometimes."

"So not all the time? When do you decide when you will do one?"

"Well some meetings I don't even get it out of the bag! When I do I write the notes into my pad then write it up when I get back."

"Nick, this is a rigid part of the process and cannot be bent. I will show you how to use the tool so that it becomes an integral part of the sales process and will help you produce more sales than actually not using it."

I said, "That would be great" but I wasn't overly convinced he could as I still had a really limiting belief about using it.

"Tell me then, Nick, how you position it with the client and also when you position it?"

"Well Pele, to be honest, I use it in the second meeting when I am presenting the products, or towards the end of the first meeting when I am getting his personal information for me to prepare the solutions."

"Nick, clearly that is your problem with using the tool. You are not using the tool, you are form filling."

He was right, I was using it just as a form to collect data about the client. I couldn't help but think that was what it was, just a form. "So when would you suggest I use it Pele?"

"Well, in the first meeting as you make the transition from **DIRECTION to DIALOGUE.**"

"You need to explain how to do that as I would never use it that early in the meeting."

"Okay Nick, let's go through it together. The tool is for collecting client information, however, it is for you to collect as much sales information as possible. You see the information as just hard facts: such as the client's age, the number of children, his or her employer etcetera. The important part is how you now use that information. So back to the transition, Nick. Remember what we discussed earlier, that everything sets up the context for the next piece."

"Yes, please explain how it works here."

"Of course I will Nick. You know when you ask the client to extend the meeting after the 10 minutes and the, ME, US, YOU?"

"Yes, of course."

"Well this is the 'tell me about you' piece."

I sat there and thought, 'Yes! Perfect'. I said, "How does that work?"

"Well Nick, I would say something like, 'Thank you for extending the meeting and for me to understand your exact requirements and really understand what's important to you, do you mind if I ask you a few questions?' He says, 'No problem, Nick'. You say, 'For me to do that and make sure I capture all the important points, I will use this form here.' I lean over the table and show him or her the different boxes and highlight the types of questions I will ask. It of course links back to the context you set right at the beginning of your call. He or she says fine and you have now introduced the form to the client."

I was impressed by how simple that was to introduce and he had reframed my fear of filling out the form. "How do you ask the questions with the form?"

"You don't ask the questions with the form, you use the stuff we have talked about earlier; the elevators, the funnel etcetera to understand the client. In other words, just because the form may say, 'Name and date of birth' at the top, you don't need to break the flow by asking him or her their name and date of birth."

"Where should I start then, Pele ?"

"Where ever the content takes you. If the client says he or she wants to talk about school fees, or whatever they want to discuss, you start there."

I could see how it was staring to come together in my mind now. It did seem simple and was a hundred times better than my present process which, Pele had already confirmed, was non existent.

"Pele, can you give me an example of some of the questions you would use?"

"Sure Nick, what questions do you normally have difficulty with?"

I immediately said, "Income. How do you ask someone how much they are earning?"

"Yes, without the right context that is always a difficult question. Let's then create a couple of contexts. Imagine you are discussing his or her school fees and, using the funnel, you get to the funding part of the schools fees. You may say something like, 'Mr X as you are aware school fees in private schools are hugely expensive; do you intend to fund them from capital or income, or perhaps both?' Let's be difficult, I intend to fund them from capital. So we still don't have the income answer do we?"

"No, we don't?"

"I can ask him, 'So how much capital do you have?' creating one funnel. Let's say he says 200k. We could say, 'so assuming 30k per annum fees that gives you just over six and half years of funding. This is great news as that means it carries your child through until University. Will you use your disposable income to save and fund the university fees as you go through school?' He might reply, 'Yes I suppose I need your help with doing that?' and I say, 'Of course, Mr X', or hopefully you are on first name terms by now Nick, 'that's what we are here to do. So that I can understand the best way to do that how much are you earning presently?' He replies without a second's thought, 'I earn Y'. 'Does that include overtime and bonuses?' 'No, bonuses are separate.' Nick, it's just structure, you know how to get to the answer, just don't panic and rush."

I made some notes and let that sink in as he went on.

"Another context could be retirement. You could say, 'Mrs Y, or Jill, if you were to retire tomorrow how much of your present salary would you need to retire on?' 'About 50% Nick.' 'Great and what is 50%, as of days value?' '40k.' 'So 80k earnings presently, does that include bonuses etcetera?'."

I suddenly had this feeling of unease come over me as it was going to be my turn soon. The thought of being on a joint call with Pele suddenly became daunting. He made it sound so simple, everything I threw at him was just water off a duck's back.

"Remember the elevators and the funnel, Nick, the rest will be easy. Nick let's just take a five minute break and then we should do the fact finding role plays. Write down practice first, though."

Practice

Pele left the room and I just sat there gazing out of the window from the couch. I put my hand into my pocket and pulled out my Blackberry to check my emails. I flicked through the inbox deleting the spam and email marketing-shots. I flicked to Outlook to check on the timings of the afternoon meeting, it was 3pm. For a split second the butterflies rose in my stomach, I so need to do this meeting well. Just as I started to feel the knot tighten, Pele came back in to the room.

"Nick, I have ordered sandwiches for lunch today as we won't have time, especially with the 3pm meeting and the role-plays we will do now." He looked at his watch and said, "I make it 11:40, they should be here around 1pm."

We spent the rest of the morning until lunch practicing communication, specifically around the way you obtain the mixture of hard and soft facts. What was really useful was the way in which the learning was coming together as I practiced. The funnels and the way I could start to group important sales information about the client actually added real flow and structure for me.

Field Visits

"Nick, I think you are ready to take this knowledge and apply it in a real sales call. Let's eat lunch now and then we can get to our first meeting."

I was starving, all this thinking had made me hungry and I was just glad the role plays were over. As I walked over to the table the sandwiches were on, Pele handed me a plate. I looked down at the wide selection and thought he had ordered enough for five people.

"I wasn't sure what you liked so I ordered a variety Nick."

"Thank you, a perfect choice", I picked up a one of each and went and sat down again on the couch.

Pele joined me. As he sat down he said, "Nick, tell me about our meeting at 3 pm?"

"What do you want to know Pele?" A question to a question, my playing for time tactic.

"Who is it? Is it a first meeting? More importantly what is the objective of this call?"

"It's a guy I met out at a networking event, he runs his own business. It's a first meeting."

"So what does his company do?"

Trying not to choke on my chicken salad sandwich, I said, "I thought that was the purpose of the meeting."

"Well Nick, if that is the purpose of the call we might as well sit here and just do the research on the internet."

I felt that defensive feeling start to wash over me again as I realised I had very little background information on the client and his company. School Boy Error, I thought. "I don't have any information on the company, Pele."

"Okay Nick, we can do that quickly after you have eaten. The purpose of the call should be a couple of things. One, to extend the meeting beyond 10 minutes. Two, to take all the information and gain commitment to a second meeting should the client have the requirements to warrant a second meeting."

"When you say warrant a second meeting, what do you mean?"

"Well Nick, he might not need our services or he might need them, but can't afford them. We will take the information and work out what's best for both him and us. It is not just about making the meeting, going along and flogging him what ever we want at a price that doesn't work. Most people require the services we offer, however, sometimes we will be unable to agree terms. We are running a business Nick, we must always remember that the client will want to drive cost down while we will always want the best margins we can get. That is also part of the flow and gaining commitment and agreeing commercially viable terms for both parties is what moves a prospect to the client list."

I agreed with him but couldn't help thinking that I could actually just do with a few sales this month, irrespective of the margins. I was so glad that Pele couldn't sense the desperation in my thoughts.

We finished eating our lunch and I used the desk top to access the company website and made as many useful notes as I could about the prospect's company. Pele just sat and watched, sipping on his sparkling water. When I had finished collating the information that might be useful in the call he looked at his watch and said, "Okay Nick, we don't want to be late so we better leave now."

I looked at my watch, it was now 2 :15. I said, "Shall we grab a cab?"

"No Nick, we can go in my car and chat on the way."

"Okay, great."

He grabbed his suit jacket from the stand and we left. We took the elevator down to the basement parking and entered the car park. The floor looked like polished concrete and as cars drove over it their tyres made a screeching sound. As we walked across the basement I started thinking, 'I wonder what car he drives?' Then I saw it. A Colbert Grey, Aston Martin DB9. The green eyed monster of jealousy was creeping into my thoughts. I had always wanted one, but it was well outside my pay scale. "Nice car."

"Thank you."

"Have you had it long?"

"No this one is new, I just swapped my old one."

I waited for him to open his door first, before opening mine, You could feel the weight in the door, it felt solid. It seemed lower and longer than I remembered. When I say remembered, I had been to the show room once and sat in one, as all sales people do, seeking inspiration. The noise as he started the car soon stopped my reminiscing as I sunk into the leather seat.

"I just love this car, Pele. I really want to get one."

"I love the experience of driving this car Nick, it is, however, only a car."

"Why did you buy it if it's only a car to you?"

"Good question Nick. I bought it for many reasons and as I say, I like the driving experience. I am in the advice business, Nick, and for people to listen to advice they generally have a confused sense of value. They believe that my advice is worth more if I am successful and to demonstrate that they expect you to have the trappings of success. Our craving in modern society is for material things to go along with fame and fortune. Twitter and social media is successful for many reasons, however part of the success is built on the concept of being able to communicate and follow the rich, the famous and the modern day idols. My point is, Nick, for me to follow my passion for coaching, I had to create a perceived success. Create a world of attachments as a way of demonstrating what I say has a material and commercial benefit. In truth, we can find that some of the best advice in life comes from the most unlikely sources and has no commercial value. Yet at the time the advice is given it means everything and creates real change in that person. What is the point in advice if it is not taken, acted on, doesn't make you think and It doesn't create change in some form?"

I was so focused on what Pele had been saying, I didn't realise we had arrived at the destination. It was the voice on the Sat Nav saying that exact phrase; 'you have arrived at your destination,' that broke my thoughts.

We parked in the visitor parking and I could feel my anxiety rising as I thought of my first client meeting with Pele. It was like being selected to play football as a kid and find yourself in the squad but on the bench. Everything is calm until the coach says Nick, warm up, your on. The excitement and anxiety of playing well, all mixed together in a pool of emotion.

Pele seemed to have an innate ability to read me. He said, "Nick you have practiced all the elements of this first meeting, now it is just the application of what you know. Let's just go and enjoy the experience of meeting someone new and interesting."

We got out of the car and walked towards the office block. As we entered the foyer, there were security staff behind the desk in the far corner, near the lifts. There was a glass panel indicating which floor for each department. It was only then I grasped the fact there was only one company in the building. I was expecting a serviced business hub with lots of companies, yet it was just the one. The realisation that I had made an appointment with the MD and owner of such an impressive business and to think, I thought it would be a serviced office but instead he owned the entire office block. I wondered whether I would have been intimidated not to call if I had known before I rang him? Pele had already spoken to the security staff as I was staring up into the glass panel like a lost school boy.

"Nick we are on the 15th floor" he said as the security guard pushed the button for the lift.

Pele and I entered the lift and as the doors closed he said, "This is a good start, Nick."

We came out of the lift to be met by our prospect's secretary who greeted us and offered us a drink. She said that James would be with us in a couple of minutes. I sat in the soft chair and was looking at the TV screen that was on silent but showing the latest news with subtitles moving across the bottom of the screen. Pele was flicking through the company literature that was on the coffee table in front of us.

James then came out of his office and greeted us. "Hi Nick, how are you doing?"

"Yes, great thanks, James" and before I could introduce him, Pele had already put his hand out and introduced himself.

James led us into his office. It was very modern yet contemporary. It was a corner office with floor to ceiling windows, modern furniture and polished wooden flooring. It was large with a board room table at the far end surrounded by cream leather seats. There was a picture on the wall of a galloping black horse with a sea of vibrant colours in the background. I stopped and looked at it for a second as James directed us to the board room table.

A man appeared with a tray and three cups of coffee, placing them on the table mats in front of each of us. We all said 'thank you' as he slipped out as quickly as he had appeared.

Over to me then I thought. I was just about to start when Pele said, "Mr Barca, thank you for taking the opportunity to see Nick and myself and before Nick starts please let me explain my role here today. I work with the company, however my role is not to advise clients but observe all our staff who interact with clients and hopefully prospective clients like yourself. Unfortunately for Nick, he gets to do this meeting today with me observing as one of his other colleagues will tomorrow. The reason for me observing today is in fact two fold; one because as a company, we believe in the ongoing development of our core staff for which Nick is one. The second is so we get to hear directly from the clients when they interact with our staff and this information is helpful when designing our customer service strategy."

"Okay, that's great Pele and thankyou for the explanation. So over to you then Nick."

"Thankyou James. As I said on the phone, I would like to talk to you about wealth accumulation. Before I do that, what I would like to do is tell you a little bit about ME, tell you a little bit about US and then it would be great if you could tell us about YOU and your successful business." I was off and running, smooth as silk.

We concluded the meeting and agreed to meet again in two days time. I was going away to put together my ideas which I would present to James and hopefully get the business. We both said goodbye to James, his secretary showing us to the lift while he went on to his next meeting.

Pele and I waited at the lift in silence and didn't say a word until we were outside. The sun was shining as we walked across the car park towards the car.

"How do you think that went, Nick?"

"Actually, I thought it went really well."

"Good, what we should do is go get a drink and do a full review."

I thought, drink? Bar? I said, "Maybe a bit early to drink."

He said, "Tea, not beer, Nick," and smiled at me.

We got in the car and drove around the corner to a little coffee shop. It was on the boulevard yet Pele quickly found a parking space right outside. As I got out I was conscious that people were looking at us and the car. The ego kicked in as we walked towards the coffee shop, taking a seat outside. I tried to imagine what it would be like to have this feeling every day if it was my car. The sun was quite strong and in my suit I really felt warm. I placed my jacket on the back of the chair undid my top button. Pele moved the umbrella around to take the sun out of our eyes then ordered tea as I people watched and day dreamed.

"Nick, I don't want to take you away from the light, or the beauty of the day, however I must change your focus now."

I said, "Sure", still watching as the beauty of the day walked by in 6 inch heals. I caught him just sitting there smiling at me. It was almost one of those father and son moments when you realise your father knows what you're thinking. As he poured our tea from the pot he said, "Focus, Nick, right here right now. Nick let's get back to James and our meeting. So give me your thoughts?"

Before I answered I could see Pele's pad open to the side of him, he had obviously taken copious notes throughout the call. I glanced down but couldn't read them upside down. Had he written good things? Certainly from my perspective it was one of my best meetings.

"I believe I did well on the ME, US, YOU. I hit my objective and got the extension from the 10 minutes to almost an hour and a half. I felt the questioning was okay. I think I have enough points to be able to put together the ideas to present to him."

"Good Nick, what do you think could have gone better?"

I never like this question, who likes admitting you made errors or did anything badly? "Perhaps, I could have summarised each funnel better. I would be interested in what you think, Pele." This was my attempt to shift the conversation back onto him, as criticism of any type is not great, especially when it comes in the form of self analysis.

Pele said, "Nick," in a soft slow tone and moved forward in his chair, resting on his arms, "remember, there is no failure, only feedback. Everything we talk about here and experienced in the meeting today, is for us both to improve. I learn from what you do, as it crystallises my thinking on what works in the process and it reinforces which pieces are not useful to us. You learn by having someone to observe you who can give you a wider view of your process because you can't be focused in the meeting and also observing yourself doing the meeting."

He of course was right. I had come up with one thing only and had generalised the overall meeting was good, so it was good to me.

"Nick, I thought it went well from an objective point of view. You were able to create enough context to maintain James' interest. You were able to extend the meeting from 10 minutes, which allowed you to obtain the information you need to prepare the sales proposal or ideas for a second meeting. Therefore as these were your sales meeting objectives, we can agree the meeting was a success."

"Great Pele, thankyou." I was feeling proud as punch now, it had all went well. I found myself drifting off to people watching again.

"You are welcome. Let's now look at your sales meeting from a structural perspective. When I say structural I mean both the process itself and how you were interacting in the process. Remember Nick selling is both an Art and a Science. Me, Us, You, went well and your statements were relevant and took into account the WIIFM concept. The control and flow was good. Rapport was maintained throughout most of the meeting and your matching and pacing were good and you built empathy with the client. You introduced the fact find well and used the overall sales funnel well. The individual funnels were good and created enough information for you to prepare your quotes and sales proposal. I agree with your point, your summary was not as strong as I would have liked. The reason I say that is because the reinforcement of the key reasons and the criteria that was important to him wasn't emphasised enough. This is likely to create some resistance in the second meeting.

"What do you mean by resistance in the second meeting?"

As you know Nick, the process is fluid and what happens in one part, directly affects another. By not gaining commitment and reinforcing the reasons and criteria today, you won't be able to use it to close the sales next time."

So what should I have done?"

"Well, as an example Nick, when you were funneling James on his life assurance and he said he agreed life insurance was important. The natural thing is to move straight on to the next question which you did. Actually, the next or follow on question was about the reason why it was important to him. He could have said, 'the reason why it is important is because my family are the whole reason I do what I do, they are completely dependant on me'. The next question Nick, could be an up or down elevator question."

I was looking at Pele and thinking I used the elevators but said nothing.

"So a question could have been, 'James if the whole reason you do what you do is creating complete dependency, what could you do differently?' Or a down elevator question could be, 'James when you say they are completely dependent, how specifically, do you feel about that?' So let's keep with the down elevator question, he may say, 'I have this underlying fear that I am not being responsible with their future'. So in your presentation, the follow on piece would be, 'James, as we sit here now, discussing your life assurance, do you recall how the whole reason for you doing what you do, is for your family? And you said that by not having the life assurance now created an underlying fear that you were not being responsible? Given this fear and your overwhelming responsibility, coupled with the success you have created through your business for your family, is there any reason why you should not start the life assurance right now?'"

I was thinking if I was James I would be getting my cheque book out and signing straight away. Pele didn't say anything, he didn't even break the flow Still sitting forward in his chair he took a sip of tea, picked up his pen and drew a straight line across the paper in front of me. He wrote **'informative'** on one end of the line and **'persuasion'** on the other end.

"Nick if you were to mark the line with a cross on it, to demonstrate where you believe you were in the meeting, where would the mark be? In other words, were you more informative or more persuasive?"

After Pele's demonstration, I looked at the line and put the x about two thirds of the way in towards where he had written 'informative'. I would have put it towards persuasion 5 minutes ago. "I would think it was about there Pele."

"Yes Nick, I think you are about right." Good I thought. Pele continued. "Nick, are you a teacher or a sales person?"

Strange question, I thought. I said, "I don't understand?"

"Well, you now have to learn that the art of selling is about persuasion, far more so than information. This is not to suggest we are not completely transparent with the prospect or client. What I am referring to here, Nick, is we must focus on how we use language to create action, in our clients and prospects. So as you sit there now Nick, listening to me talking, listening to the feedback on this meeting, you realise that you are able to persuade anyone on anything. As you think about that now, with the sun on your face , as you sit there, it is conformation that the true art of selling is persuasion and you have that skill don't you?"

I said, "Yes" without thinking. It didn't feel pushed to say yes, it was almost trance like as he said it in one almost continuous flow of words. "What just happened?"

"That was an example of Verbal pacing and leading, Nick and it is used as a technique to persuade and influence people."

I was intrigued almost excited. "How does it work, Pele? Can I use it all the time in any context?"

"Now, to answer your question Nick, some people use it as a tool and switch it on and off as a way to get what they want. The focus is on themselves, not the other person. It is, I win, you lose. Other people use it to build better relationships and use it to get what they want but their intention is a win/win approach."

Pele had raised his voice and sped up his tone. It was like a light coming on, I just recognised it for the first time. He had just paced me and as he lowered his voice, I calmed down instinctively. I had just been lead.

"So can it be used in any context? Yes, everything is a transferable skill, Nick. My point is, Nick, what is your intention when you use it? Verbally pacing and leading someone for the wrong reason is actually more difficult as the energy between you is still not flowing and therefore is solely reliant on the language patterns. So to use it in a busy bar or club would be more difficult, if that is the intention behind the question."

My original thought had been about using it in the bars and clubs and so I certainly wasn't in the win/win camp. It was like he just read my mind, it was scary. The waiter came over and asked if we needed anything else? Pele put his hand on his pot and asked for two more pots of tea as they had gone cold. As the waiter walked away, Pele looked at me, his eyes cutting through me. It was a strange feeling, almost piercing but still soft as he said, "Nick, you have real ability to create greatness and your underlying spirit demands it from you. You are far greater than your thinking. I am here to guide you to greatness, to your true self. I will show you how to get there, yet it is for you to demonstrate it in everything you do. Every breath you take, Nick, feeds your soul and as you inhale and exhale now, your words and thoughts flow out as the wind into the process of life. Make them both worthy."

The emotion suddenly welled up in me. I felt I had let him down, let myself down. I knew I had to control my thoughts by changing my behaviour as I really want to be true to myself and be the best I can be. The waiter returned with the two pots of tea and put them down in front of us. I didn't look up as I was staring at my note pad, still reflecting on the emotions and thoughts running through me. Pele broke my train of thought when he said he had poured my tea. I shook it off mentally and put sugar in my cup, then stirred. The simple, familiar actions returned me to some semblance of equilibrium.

He smiled at me and said, "Right, let's get back to the feed-back from the meeting. Then we will look at Persuasion and Influence and some of the other key pieces you will need to get James to take action and do the business with us. Is that Okay?"

"Yes, Pele, that's perfect."

"The other key piece of the first meeting which you missed was the referrals, Nick."

"Sorry Pele, but I never ask for referrals in the first meeting. I would think that is really pushy."

"Actually Nick, it is the best time to ask for them."

"How do you do that and why?" Mentally, I was really not in agreement with Pele on this.

"Well Nick, there was a wonderful book written by Dr Robert Cialdini called the *'Influence the Psychology of Persuasion'* which he wrote in 1984. It highlights six principles of influence, which actually, Nick, is a perfect segue into referrals and why you would ask for them in the first meeting."

I opened my notepad as this was going to be interesting. I wrote in the margin **'Get Pele to do verbal pacing and leading again'**, next to the book reference about Dr Robert Cialdini.

"So let me answer your question. When you are doing the overall summarising of the meeting Nick, you need to lay out the next stage of the process with the client and set his or her expectations. They need to know, exactly what will happen next and what, if anything, they need to do themselves. This is professional and adds to your credibility, it also shortens your sales cycle."

"I don't understand what you mean by shortening the sales cycle, Pele?"

"Well let's say you need proof of Identification. You might say, 'James, should you like my ideas and decide they are worth doing, I will need a copy of your passport as well as your utility bill as part of the summary'. If you don't do that Nick then it is likely he will not have it with him in the next meeting and then you will need a third trip just to complete the paper work. Of course any delay in the process can impact on credibility and could lead to the client changing his mind and doing the business with someone else."

I thought I never do this properly, sometimes I am just wanting to finish the meeting quickly because I have the belief the prospect will be in a hurry to finish the meeting.

"You do the same with the referrals however, you don't take them."

"I don't get that. You ask for them but don't take them?"

"No Nick, you don't take them. You see the six principles Nick, well one of those principles is 'commitment and consistency'. What Dr Cialdini says is we have a deep routed desire to be consistent and if we say to someone we will do something we are more likely to do it. So in line with this principle and in the context of referrals in the first meeting, please imagine this follows on from what I just said Nick, you would say something like this, 'So, James, I will need a copy of your passport as well as your utility bill. Also James, could you do me a favour? Between now and next week when we meet, could you think of which of your business associates might be interested in the services we offer?' Now, because it is next week it is non threatening. He will likely say, 'Yes, sure no problem'. According to the consistency principle what comes next Nick?"

"I still don't see how it works, Pele."

"So okay. Look, in the summary when you see James next week, what you say is, 'Thank you for doing the business with me James', then talk him through the next part of the process that will now follow. Once that is finished, you say, 'James, if you recall, when we spoke last week, you said you would give me the names of some of your business associates that might be interested in the service we offer. So who is it you know James, that you feel is worth me talking too?' Then Nick, you shut up and say nothing."

"Does that really work? It sounds so simple."

"It is simple and it does work because of the principle of 'commitment and consistency'. The response does vary between clients. Some will be reticent to give you more than one person, some will give you four or five. Once they have given you a name, or a few names the next piece of the process is to say, 'James, thankyou for giving me Nigel and Grant's names and contact details, I will call them over the next few days. However, before I do that, most of my clients prefer to call them first themselves and tell them that I will be calling them. Is that okay ?' Usually he'll say, 'Yes sure, I can call them'. 'As I only want 10 minutes of their time James, it will be easy for me to fit it around their schedule, whatever time suits pretty much. Thankyou again for the business and speaking to Nigel and Grant and I will be I touch over the next few weeks'. Then finish the meeting Nick and over the next couple of days ring them. Interestingly, what I find is that the client not only tells the referral that you will call, he will also tell him you are a nice guy and they should give you the 10 minutes. The fact that a peer or someone they know has called them and said you are a nice guy and they should see you, goes a long way to another principle of influence called '**Social Proof**'. People like to do what other people do and say is good. So part of social proof Nick, is James will probably say he has meet you and he thinks they should too. Also he might give a product endorsement for you, by saying he has bought a product himself. See, what we must do if we want the client to do something for us is to be sure to let them see other people are already doing it and they should do it too. They need to see that others like them, or people with perceived better standing in the community, believe in your product and are using it. It's called '**Liking**'. Remember the old saying, people buy from people they like? Another principle is liking. It is an obvious one, however Nick, it is also about the prospects believing you are like them as a person. This is where the techniques of body language and communication come in as increases in rapport between you. So what it should say is, people buy from people who they like and are perceived to be like them."

That made perfect sense and it was something I knew I reacted too, so why not a prospect?

"**Authority** is the next principle. People will always listen to someone who they believe is an authority on a subject. That's why it is important when you do the 'Me, Us, You' that you created an Authority Statement Nick, as it starts the meeting highlighting why they should listen."

I sat there writing, listening and thinking how it all made sense. I was seeing the overall process in my head and for the first time, I was actually thinking I could get to do this job well.

"**Scarcity** is another principle, Nick. It is used to make the client take action because they believe the product or offer is scarce. So an example is next week you could say to James, 'I know you want to do this Life Assurance however it's not actually up to you or I, it is up to underwriting and they may decide you can't have it. So we don't waste time, we should complete the forms and submit the application to see if you can'. Sometimes Nick, when we run those product offers that give enhanced investment allocations if the client does it this month only can they get the extra money added to the plan."

I never thought about the product offers in that way, however now Pele said it, I thought it was quite clever.

"The last one is **Reciprocity**. As the saying goes, what we send out we get back, we reap what we sow. In simple terms Nick, if you smile at someone, they smile back. If you are kind to someone they are generally kind back. So this why people give free stuff away online; such as free information, if they want to buy that type of product, they feel they should buy it from you. It is about giving or creating **Value** and giving it first so they are more likely to reciprocate when you ask them to do something for you." Pele, looked down at his notes and said, "I think we are finished here today, Nick. I think the overall meeting went well and apart from the summarising in each section and the overall summary at the end, it was a good first meeting."

"Thankyou," I said. I thought I will definitely add the summarising to my process. I said, "Asking for referrals in the first meeting was a great lesson for me Pele as I would never have done that. I also found your explanations of Dr Cialdini's principles interesting and thought I would buy the book on the weekend."

Pele paid the bill and we walked back to the car. It had been a long day and a wave of tiredness hit me. I got into the car and sank down into the leather upholstery which gave the car it's nice smell and closed my eyes to relax for just a moment.

Pele, said, "I will give you a lift home, to save you getting a cab from the office."

"You don't have too, Pele" I said, really thinking that would be nice, especially as it was in the Aston.

The sun was just going down and the air had cooled from earlier in the day. Pele pushed the button and the roof went smoothly back into the gap behind my head. As he drove I could really feel the power and the noise as we rushed along the motorway. The wind in my hair felt great. I thought 'this is the life'. The lift home wasn't long enough, but had seemed shorter mentally and it is true what they say, that time seems to go much faster when you are enjoying yourself.

I was getting out of the car when Pele said, "See you in the office tomorrow at 8am. We will do the next section of the process, **DECISIONS.** We will look at it in depth Nick, and that will also set you up for your second meeting with James. Also, Nick, promise me that tonight you will spend 15 minutes meditating in your head on the key learnings from today."

"I will Pele." I thought I really wanted James as a client so tomorrow I will need to be focused. I couldn't help but think how hard I had worked so far this week and couldn't wait to get in and relax. Pele waved and drove off. I could hear the deep roar of the Aston going up the road and away from the apartment block. As the lobby doors slid shut behind me it was like the end of another phase of the process.

Chapter 4 Decisions

'All decisions have a cost, but what is the cost of doing nothing?'
Pele Sarsson

I was up early in the morning and as I got in the shower I was feeling motivated and really positive. As the hot steam rose and filled the cubicle, so my enthusiasm for seeing Pele for my next sales fix seemed to rise, too. As I stared down at the shower tray and the hot water hit the back of my neck, I was visualising the key pieces of the structure and my overall interaction with Pele and James yesterday. As the pictures of yesterday ran through my head it was really clear in my mind. I wondered whether the 15 minutes of meditation last night had actually helped reinforce the clarity. Thirty minutes later I was caught up in the usual ritual of waiting for the lift when a new neighbour came out and started waiting with me. "Good morning" I said.

"Good morning, you're up early. I am your new neighbour."

"Nice to meet you."

"So what gets you up so early this morning?"

My thoughts went into a default of aloofness and ambiguity. "I am off to work."

He pressed on with the questioning, "so what do you do?"

I was just about to say 'I am in finance' to cut the conversation short when I heard Pele in my head. Then a strange thing happened. I said, "Actually I help people accumulate wealth" and my mood lifted. "What do you do?"

He said, "I am in advertising."

Before we knew it, the elevator had arrived. We got in and continued chatting and I found myself thinking of Pele's elevators and the fact I had been in the down elevator for a long time before the real one had arrived. By the time the lift door opened again I knew his job, company and had an overview of the advertising industry. We both said goodbye and I promised to call him. I looked down at his card in my hand and couldn't help thinking that my default position had been to be aloof towards him. What had changed my behaviour in that moment? Had the structure helped lift me out of that default position? Had the structure acted as the trigger? Was it the words, 'I help people accumulate wealth' or was it Pele's voice in my head that had made me want to be the best I can be? Either way, what ever had happened I had a new neighbour that could be a friend and a client. I was feeling good as I got in the cab and headed for the office. If only I could feel like this every morning, I thought as I stared out at the passing traffic. Pele had become this little voice in my head as I suddenly found myself asking, 'what stops me being like this every second of every day?'

I was still contemplating this question as I arrived at the office and the cab driver asked for the fare. I paid him, got out and made my way to Pele's office, the smell of the fresh coffee was almost an anchor for my interactions with him. I walked into his office as his door was open and he was on the sofa reading the financial times. He was immaculately dressed as usual. He looked over the top of his paper as I entered. "Morning Nick, hope you are well and ready for a busy day?"

"Morning Pele, yes I am really well and looking forward to it." I then launched into what had happened at the apartment. I explained how it was strange how my neighbour had appeared and we had got talking and I had recalled my learning from the last two days.

After I had finished Pele gave me one of his looks before saying, "That's excellent Nick. Before we chat, let's have a coffee and conclude your elevator story with an interesting concept first talked about by a gentleman called Carl Jung."

I sat down and listened like a little boy listening to his grandfather.

"Carl Jung came up with concept known as 'synchronicity' and Arthur Koestler in his book, *Roots of Coincidence* both talked about the relationship between occurrences or coincidences that are not causal in nature, that manifest into meaningful related events. So as I have said from day one, Nick, we are all operating in a much bigger energy framework than ourselves. In science it has a more literal translation and is described as two rays of light coming together in the same spot. Arthur Koestler said that *'we observe a large number of uncertainties producing a certainty, a large number of chance events creating a lawful total outcome'."*

I was listening and trying to put it into a sales context as Pele talked.

"Carl Jung believed that life was not actually a series of random events; in fact it was all part of a bigger system that created order. He also believed that synchronicity had a purpose of shifting a person's consciousness to the greater whole and understanding. It's funny Nick, because you can view life's coincidences and synchronicity in different ways. We normally only see the coincidences when they are completely starling and obvious to us. Does that mean they don't exist all the time and we just don't notice them? Or was it that you were sending out positive energy and meeting this new prospect came from that positive energy, attracting a different type of coincidence into your life?"

I thought about that for a moment and it seemed to be true in a weird way. When I am in a bad mood things just don't go right for me. This morning I had been in a really positive mood which made it stranger and some way feel even more real.

Pele said, "As Lewis Carroll wrote; 'it's a poor sort of memory that only works one way'. My personal experience, Nick, is that the more I send positive energy out into the bigger system the more I notice positive synchronicity in my life. The opposite is true, also. The more I send negativity out the more I get synchronicity that is negative. So whether you believe Jung's work is for you to decide but for me, living as if it is true has seemed to bring me better outcomes. I do believe we are all part of the bigger frame work of energy and whether synchronicity is the way in which that energy pulls us and events together is a interesting phenomena."

He stood up and got his pad and pen from his desk and said, "Right, Nick, let's talk about the next part of the process. I call this part of the process, '**DECISIONS**' because it is the time we are going to get the client to decide on whether he or she is going to buy now, later or never. Either way, we will get ourselves into a position of understanding as to the client's decisions."

I wrote in my note pad:

Decisions

Pele said, "Of course with Decisions comes the **Decision Making Process (DMP)** and doing what you do for the client is definitely a rational and emotional cognitive process. Ultimately Nick, we all look at alternative scenarios or ideas with the outcome of making a choice. Part of the sales process, as you know Nick, is the funneling process which you did with James yesterday. In the first part of the meeting we use this questioning technique to check the clients assumptions, also to explore the alternative scenarios in the client's mind. We then take the down elevators, as you know, to gain the client's or prospect's commitment to a series of possible alternatives. We continue to gain understanding through establishing the criteria around each alternative, until we arrive at the best agreed solution. When, this is done, we come away and put together our ideas around the agreed solution. The one thing I would remind you of Nick, is don't forget that when we talk about criteria, criteria in itself is complex. It can be emotional criteria, behavioural criteria or even intellectual criteria and as we funnel we add the criteria as an overlay of the decisions. We also add the values that are underlying the client's thinking. All of this information will add depth to your presentation and will get James or another prospect to say yes."

"Now Nick, if we can do this, in a well structured and comprehensive way in the first meeting, we should make the second meeting really easy. The reason being, you are just confirming what the client told you in terms of buying criteria. This also means you are just presenting what they told you the product would need to look like in structure. You are also reminding them of the values and criteria; that should mean they are in complete agreement."

"So structurally, when you start the second meeting, it is important to do a full recap on the first meeting. Everything I told you over the last couple of days applies, Nick. You have to start the second meeting as if it was the first again. Clearly, you don't need to do the Me, Us, You, etcetera. However you do need to focus on re-establishing rapport and getting James, or any new client, back into the frame of mind in which you left him last time you met. Personally Nick, I mentally work on the basis that the meeting never ended. It is as if I just popped out to the toilet as it creates a better perceptual position for me personally."

I just listened because as I am now so far off my old process I don't have anything to add at this stage.

"There are some key things we do need to check in our second meeting. The first is what I call 'The Same Test'. You need to say to James and or any other client or prospect a question early in the meeting. That question is, 'Since we last met, James, and giving all the information you gave me, has anything changed?' Normally he will say, 'No, Nick, everything is the same'. If however, they say, 'Actually, yes, something has changed', what do you do?"

"I would stop presenting and go into the funnel with, 'For me to understand what has changed, do you mind if I ask you a question?'."

"That's excellent Nick. That will work and then you are into a new meeting. If the thing that has changed is not major, you might be able to present the solution. If it is a major issue then don't present, take the information and come away and create some new ideas given the new information. Always remember, Nick, you are either in a first meeting or presenting in a second meeting. If you are not presenting an agreed solution you're in a first meeting, even if it is your third meeting. Conceptually it is two extensions of the first meeting."

I had never thought of it in that way before, but he was right and in the past I would be presenting because it was a second meeting and I would be in a rush to close the business.

"So, let's say there are no changes and everything is the same, Nick. What do you do after we have got back into the meeting and James is comfortable? When a prospect considers buying a product for the first time, what is the first thing he or she does Nick?"

"I don't know Pele. I would ask my mates, I think and look it up on the internet."

"That's correct, Nick. Outside of your own experience you must seek external information, the prospect or client will actively seek information. Now some people are happy to do this by researching it all themselves. Others will ask their friends and or trusted advisers about whether they have any experience of the product. What they are in fact doing, is creating a subjective position or experience on the product. There was an Indian philosopher, Krishnamurti, that said, 'the description is not the described, it is like a man who is hungry being told all about the food, having it described in every way, yet he is still hungry'. How does the client really understand life insurance when it is a promise to pay out on his or her death? It is important that we understand and where it is not aligned, challenge this subjectivity."

Once again, my head was spinning as I turned over what Pele was telling me about decisions and decision making. It seemed like he had an answer for everything, but not in some sarcastic, know-all way. My mind formed the word 'wisdom' and for the first time in my life I think I began to grasp the difference between knowledge and wisdom.

"Nick, I think it is important we chat about presenting information as a carry on from what I have already told you. We should consider its application with clients and prospects using a well known rule. This rule applies whether you are in a one to one meeting or in a stand up presentation. The is rule is known as the **'Rule of 3'**."

I wrote:

Rule of 3

"In Latin, Nick, there is a saying, '*Omne trium perfectium*'; 'everything that comes in three's is perfection'. Also, Lewis Carroll wrote in '*Hunting the Snark*', 'just the place for a snark! I have said it twice: that alone should encourage the crew. Just the place for a snark! I have said it thrice: what I tell you three times is true.' The Rule of 3 is a pattern that creates progression in our minds. It fits with what we talked about earlier with short term memory and three pieces of information. That helps clients through re-call, repetition, and reinforcing. So you could say, Nick, that giving information in chucks of three is more beneficial to our clients. It helps them **recall** what we have told them, they are then able to **repeat** it so that it **reinforces** your points and the fact that what they are doing makes complete sense to them. Don't you agree Nick?"

"Yes Pele, sounds good to me."

"Nick, presentations need to have three things; **interest, desire** and **action**. So what I am saying is, *your* presentations, Nick, need to be interesting. You must create *desire* and the prospect must take *action* after you present. There have of course been so many examples through history of the rule of three."

"Examples from history?" I was generally intrigued as I had not heard about the Rule of 3 before.

"Well Nick, the Holy Trinity; God, the Son and the Holy Spirit. Mind, body and spirit. Life, liberty and the pursuit of happiness. I came, I saw, I conquered. See? There are many more, Nick.

"Do you have anything a bit more modern Pele?"

He smiled. "If you are selling a house Nick, what do they say are the three most important things?"

Without thinking I blurted out, "location, location, location."

"Well done, are you selling a house Nick?"

"No I am not."

"But you remembered it!"

He was sharp as a razor; so much so, I reminded myself, that no matter what I think I know, there is always something to be learned.

"So let's focus on James for a minute. What information did he give you in the meeting?"

I pulled out my notes that I had taken with my funnels and read it to myself before answering. "Well Pele, he said he wanted life insurance because he had an underlying fear of being responsible and the fact he had worked hard to build the business for his family."

"So Nick, you have put together your illustrations and information about the product. How will you now present them? Let's do a role play. I will be the client and you can present them to me. Nick, just present the product to me, there is no need for you to do the overall recap."

I was right on the spot and could suddenly feel an immediate pressure when he said that. I fumbled around pulling the papers together, trying to get them into some resemblance of order. "Right then, Pele" I said, "I will present the product to you. Pele, you said you wanted to buy life assurance so let me tell you about what I have done for you. You said you needed $ 500,000 of life cover and you wanted to do it as cheaply as possible to protect your family."

"Yes I did Nick."

"Well, I believe the cheapest way for you to do that Pele, is to do term assurance. I have put together some alternatives for you to consider. You can get $500,000 as you requested for $1,000 dollars per month, which is within your budget, to protect your family. The other alternative is you can pay annually which works out about $1000 per annum cheaper."

"Thank you, Nick, I will look at these and go through them later in detail."

I recognised the objection and realised I was faced with overcoming it. "Well Pele, perhaps, we should go through them in detail now, so that I can explain them so you can really understand what you are buying?"

Pele smiled, "Okay Nick, let's stop the role play for a minute. Let's revisit where we are and what we should be doing. Firstly, Nick, check your language; you need to use words that are motivating and or positive."

"What do you mean?" I asked for an example.

"Sure Nick. There is a difference between **Cost** and **Value**. 'Cheapest' might have been the word he used but in this case when you are presenting you should reframe this for the client. See Nick, if the client says 'cheapest', he or she probably means they are thinking of a budget and getting the best value for their money. We all want to do a deal do we not?"

It was a rhetorical question and he carried on.

"This is also suggesting that he might think that the product is mentally a cost to him for which he has no benefit. Why? Because he will be dead so the benefit is for someone else. So I would suggest to start you should say something like, 'James, I know when we spoke you were conscious of getting the best value for your money before you would consider buying the life assurance. You said, after we had looked at all your outgoings and after much consideration, that provided I could do it within the agreed amount of a $1000 per month it would be fine. You also said that $500k death benefitwould be enough to protect your family should anything happen to you. Nick, so as agreed, I have got you $500k worth of life assurance that will protect your family if you die and it will go someway to discharging that feeling of responsibility that you hold as a husband and father. I have also been able to create all of this life cover within the budget you gave me of a thousand dollars per month as agreed. Nick, do you have any questions before I fill out the forms?"

I wanted to give him the same answer as he had given me. I threw out the objection of, "I want to think about it Pele". I just wanted to be clever to see what he did.

He smiled at me. "Nick, okay let's play on, if it amuses you, especially as we are in learning environment. Nick, Think about what specifically?"

Argh! The down elevator again. It was a very direct question, which threw me. I blurted out, "Is it the best alternative for me Pele? Perhaps I should shop around?" I was deliberately being difficult to him yet he was still smiling.

"So Nick, to answer your two questions, is it the best alternative for you? Yes. And should you shop around? No."

I was struggling with his direct linguistic answer to my question. It left me no margin to grab on to anything else. I kept going to annoy him though. "Why not Pele? I think I should."

"Nick, are you telling me you will get ten people to come and see you and carry out the same process as I have done?"

"Maybe not ten but a few more."

"You agreed that I understood your exact requirements, that is correct isn't it?"

"Yes you did Pele."

"And assuming this stream of others do also, they will take numerous hours of your time to come back with 500k of life cover at 1000 dollars of premium, is that correct?"

I said nothing and just looked at him. I was snookered.

"So, apart from your right to shop around Nick, I absolutely see no benefit to you for shopping around other than to come to the conclusion before you now that it is the best alternative and so not worth shopping around. My suggestion is, Nick, we should go ahead as agreed."

"I just said, "Yes that's fine."

"Nick the learning here is that it demonstrates the reasons why you must get a real understanding of the client's motives and reasons for why they want to buy the product. Another way to think about it is, 'What is the clients pain?' What does the client gain in his or her decision? Most clients make emotional decisions Nick, then reverse engineer the logic into the emotional choice they have made. Part of the problem you encountered in the role play came from you not having sufficient information about the client's motives that you could use to make the client take action. Nick, another way to think about motivation, is it is the motive that a client will take action on. It is not enough to just be matching the high level product requirements to the high level needs, which you just did."

It almost felt like a criticism as Pele was direct, but I hope not frustrated, with me. I could, however, understand what he was saying as I generally always thought of it as matching the high level client need to the product.

"Most resistance comes from lack of understanding of the client and then trying to match the high level needs you discuss to the high level features of the product. Nick let's take a quick break and I will get the coffee before we talk about features and benefits."

I made a quick note in the pad on **Features** and **Benefits**. When the coffee was ready Pele brought over the two cups and placed them on the table in front of us. He then sat down and said, "Nick, what do you know about features and benefits?"

"I was told, Pele, it is what the product is."

"And what is a benefit?"

"It is what the product does for the client."

"Okay Nick that is great. A feature is best thought of as a characteristic of the product. Take your life assurance plan, it has waiver of premium on it doesn't it?"

"Yes it does."

"So this is a feature of the life assurance product because it is a characteristic of it. Even though you could say as you did, it is what the product is. A really good thing to do Nick, is to sit down and take each product line you sell and list out the features and the benefits and consider what client needs those features met."

That seemed logical and I wondered why I had not done that already. 'Seat of the pants', the little voice in my head said.

"Do you want to practice a few Nick?"

"What, in role play?"

"Well it doesn't have to be in role play, just give me a few features and then play the benefit statement for me."

"Yes sure, I am happy to do that," so I wrote a few features down across a few different products that we offer and tried them out on Pele. "Pele, You mentioned earlier that you have no pension provision and should you be disabled before you reach retirement it would be a real problem for you, is that correct?" I paused to give him a chance to either correct me or agree.

Pele was in good form because he said, "Yes Nick that is correct."

Then I gave him the benefit statement, "Well, Pele, you'll have the security of knowing that your retirement will be safe should you take the pension with disability benefits. What that will mean is you can still enjoy your retirement even if you have to retire early through disability."

"That was good Nick. Some people also think of it as **FAB**; which is **Feature Advantages Benefits,** which is the same thing except they find it by using a, 'so what that means to you is' statement. 'So what the advantage of that to you, Nick, is...' It mentally makes you create a linking statement between the feature and the benefit."

"Pele, I have a question for you about multiple product closes. Simply put, how you do them?"

"That's a good question, Nick. Selling more than one product has its own structure. When you are closing multiple products in one meeting, you must do them individually. So using James as the example, you would close the life assurance and complete the paper work. Then you would close the pension and complete the paper work. Then the school fees and do the paper work. The process will be the same for each product, you have funneled each product and understood the needs and wants of the client. You know the emotional reasons that will motivate James on each product, so the process it is the same for each as if it was a single sale."

"Pele what happens if the client objects to one of the products?"

"Nick, firstly clients don't object, they are demonstrating some level of resistance to buying your product through a lack of understanding. It is either they don't understand something about the product or you have failed to understand what they want. Anyway, let me answer the direct question for you Nick. So, how do you handle client resistance? Firstly, there is a structure for handling objections and you'll never guess what? It starts with the funnel Nick!" He said it in a jovial way, almost smiling at himself as he said it. "I do like to keep things simple Nick."

I said, "I am glad, simple works for me Pele. I was thinking, it is hard enough remembering what to say let alone thinking about, structures in structures."

"What I will say, Nick, is at the top of the resistance funnel there is one question that is important. You can get Mr X to acknowledge the issue and then isolate the objection by saying, 'Mr X, apart from your concerns about Y, are you happy with the rest of what we have talked about?' He says, 'Yes, the rest is fine, Nick'. You have now isolated the objection. Now, using the funnel we say, 'For me to understand your concerns about Y, do you mind if I ask you a few questions?' and you are off and running."

"What if there is more than one objection, Pele?"

He looked at me smiling and said, "You're in deep trouble!" He then said, "You still isolate them, Nick. You deal with each objection separately and gain commitment to move on. Once you have funneled each objection to understand the issue, deal with it and move to the next. Only after the client agrees you have dealt with his or her concerns. Once you have dealt with the concerns you should now move to filling out the paper work. Some people call this the assumed close. I think of it as the natural progression in the process. Nick, if you have done your job properly and gained commitment throughout the process and built a real understanding of the prospect or client so you understand their requirements, their needs and wants, you should seldom get any resistance. Which brings us to the last part of the process, the piece I call, **Delivery**."

I wrote **DELIVERY** in my note book.

Chapter 5 Delivery

'Your work is going to fill a large part of your life, and the only way to be truly satisfied is to do what you believe is great work'
Steve Jobs

"I call it delivery because it is exactly that, it is when you have to deliver on those promises. Nick it is so important nowadays for all organisations to have a robust post sales process and effective CRM system. I am not going to talk about the use of the internal CRM system and or the pros and cons of which system as there are so many variations on the market. I am more interested in talking about doing regular customer visits and things that I believe add value and build depth to your relationship with your clients. It is also important to remember, that delivery is in fact the starting point of the next sale."

"How does that work Pele? I was always taught it is post sales because it is the end of the cycle."

"No Nick, it is the end of that one sale, that one interaction with that one client. It is a continuous process and as I mentioned before, work with the presupposition that all your meetings are continuations of your previous meetings. Every client meeting is an opportunity to do more business. So imagine Nick, a client like James needs to save twenty thousand dollars per annum to retire at 60. He can only afford ten thousand now. What do you do?"

"I would try and make him do twenty, Pele."

"Yes agreed, perhaps the best time you can do that is on an annual review."

"How would I do that?"

"What you must do is after you have made the sale and collected the paper work, you must frame it. Would you like an example?"

"For sure, Pele."

"Let's use James as an example then. 'James, in conclusion, thank you for trusting me to look after your financial requirements. As we mentioned earlier, I always do an annual review with my clients and I would like to set that with you today, if that works for you?' I then put it in my diary Nick. Then continue with, 'As a trusted advisor to you on your financial matters, it would be remiss of me not to remind you that you are underfunding your pension requirements by ten thousand dollars per year. When we meet next and, provided you are still happy and the level of service I offer is in line with your needs, then James I will be wanting to close the gap between ten thousand and the twenty thousand that you require to retire at 60. Are you okay with that?' He says, 'Yes'. Now when you meet again we are back to my friend Robert Cialdini and consistency."

"So what do you say then?"

"You say, 'If you recall James, last time we met I told you I would want to close the gap between the ten and twenty thousand and you said you were okay with that. So how closer can you get James?'."

"It sounds to easy Pele, is it really that simple?"

"Yes Nick. I like the quote by Edsger Wybe Dijkstra."

'Simplicity is a great virtue but it requires hard work to achieve it and education to appreciate it. And to make matters worse: complexity sells better.'

"The best sales people that I know working within your sector Nick, usually do an annual review with all of their clients as a minimum. They do a first follow up in the First Quarter as a confirmation that the decision the client made to become a client was the right one. Nick, Lots of sales are actually lost in the first month because clients fear they have made the wrong choice. Their friends may also create uncertainty, all of which are normal occurrences within the sales cycle. This is why it is so important to deepen your relationships with each client. Why should you do that? Because you need to move from being a sales person into a trusted advisor. Nick what is one of the largest costs in any business?"

"I don't know, salaries?"

"Actually Nick, I was thinking of client acquisition. Businesses spend millions on getting new clients, creating complex marketing strategies and enhancing brand recognition, all in an attempt to get new clients. When, interestingly, it is accepted that more than fifty percent of sales come from the word of mouth of existing clients. My experience has been that the value of the transaction actually increases, the better the quality of the referral from a satisfied client. Also the speed of the transaction is quicker, cutting sales lead times and enhancing profits."

That made sense, I thought, if only on how much time each sales person spent prospecting and going through the whole process of making appointments, chasing leads and so on. How great would it be if half my new leads called me!

"Nick, **Referrals** and word of mouth introductions are the bulls eye of prospecting. The greater your relationship and influence with your clients, the greater your ability to never have to cold call again. Prospecting becomes a process of meeting with people who just want to do business. Nick, what would it be like not to have to prospect again other than through direct client referrals?"

"It would be great Pele, in fact it would be brilliant, as without doubt, prospecting is the worse part of the job."

"Then how long will it take you to get three hundred and sixty five clients?"

"I don't know, Pele, two years? Why?"

"The reason why is because, if you have three hundred and sixty five clients that's one meeting a day which should result in a top up sale. Also it should lead to at least one new referral from your existing client. It's so simple it's scary, Nick."

I thought about what he said, it did seem really simple.

"Nick, two years is fine and if it isn't, then you have a choice. Either speed up the sales cycle or accept that it will be hard work prospecting until you have three hundred and sixty five clients. So to speed it up what I want you to think about is; how do you become a trusted advisor to your clients and move away from being perceived as just the sales guy? That's the other part of **Delivery;** it is the realisation that as soon as you have a client you can make the move from sales person to trusted advisor in the eyes of the client. It is all down to you and the ongoing service and advice you deliver to your clients."

"I'm not certain that I really know what a trusted advisor means Pele."

"Yes Nick, it does mean different things to different people. However, one thing that everyone agrees on is, that trusted advisors have reached a position of substantial influence over their clients. To do so, you have to demonstrate you are a superior practitioner. That you continually demonstrate high integrity, commitment and someone that clients can have complete faith in within their profession. It is this, that you should strive for, Nick."

"Sounds like a saint, Pele."

He laughed and said, "Yes Nick, outside of its religious connotations, a saint is someone who is always virtuous, has a strong moral compass and is valued by everyone. Question is Nick, can you be a saintly sales person? Can you really grasp the **Spirit of Selling**?" He smiled. "Truly enlightened, a continuous demonstration of virtue, a real trusted advisor?"

I sat and contemplated Pele's question. I looked down at my note pad trying to find inspiration, an answer to his question. My thoughts were racing round my head. Would I really have the self discipline it would take? Can I create a set of values that I can live by that would make me a trusted adviser to my clients?"

Pele said, "Nick, I want to tell you a story."

It broke my thought pattern, a relief from my self analysis.

"There was once a young boy that wanted to be man, a fisherman like his father. He would sit on the dock of the bay and watch his father working away on his boat. His father would be working hard, preparing his nets, preparing the boat. Making sure that the boat was ready to deliver him his bounty from the sea. His precise and dedicated preparation would take hours everyday. The boy, would ask his father, 'why father do you prepare for so long everyday? The weather is good, why don't you and I just go out and catch fish?' His father would smile at him and say, 'My son, when you know the answer to your question we will go fishing. The boy would always ask the same question and his father would say the same thing to him. My son, when know the answer to your question we will go fishing. Time passed and the boy got older and, he believed, more experienced and he watched his father and said, 'Father, I know the answer to the question, it's because you can catch more fish'. 'No, my son, when you know the answer to the question we can go fishing. The boy was now a man and one day his father said, 'Son, we should go fishing.' The boy was shocked. He said, 'Father, I don't know the answer to the question and we are going fishing?' 'Yes my son, we will fish today.' The young man was excited as they got in the boat. He noticed the wind was up as they left the port. The excitement of being a man now and being in the boat, leaving port for the first time, it felt great. The sails caught the wind and they were on their way. 'Father where are we going fishing?' 'Does it matter where we go my son?' The boy said, 'Well no, actually father I am happy to just go where the wind takes me.' 'Then my son, that's what we will do, we will go where the wind blows us.' Time was passing and the boy said, 'Father, how long until I can catch some fish?' 'Well my son, I thought we were just letting the wind blow through the sails and take us where it takes us. Are you not enjoying the experience of fishing?' The boy thought about the question, 'Father I am not aware of the experience, as I am so focused on getting to the spot where we can fish.' The father smiled, 'My son change your focus, feel the wind in your hair, the spray on your face, it is all part of what it is to go fishing.' The boy, looked out to sea, over the front of the boat and could see the swell rising up and the small boat was now pitching and water was coming over the boat. 'Father, water is coming over the boat and the boat is pitching hard.' 'Yes my son, I thought you wanted to fish, are you not enjoying the experience of fishing?' The boy thought about it and said, 'Father I am not thinking of the experience of fishing, I am now focused on the swell and the fear of the water coming over the boat.' 'My son the swell and the fear of the water coming over the front of the boat is all part of fishing. I thought you wanted to go fishing, are you not enjoying fishing with me?' 'Father, I am not certain now I want to fish, perhaps I am not cut out to be a fisherman.' 'My son, when the fear builds and the water comes over the boat and your focus is now on self doubt, does that mean you are not enjoying the fishing?' The boy thought about the question, 'No father, it means I am not fishing, I am doing something else.' The weather suddenly changed and the sun came out and the sea calmed. The boy grabbed the nets and threw them over the side of the boat. He could suddenly feel the heat of the sun on him, he took his shirt off and lay down in the boat. 'Father, this is what I think of when I think of fishing, this is perfect.' 'My son, the things you experienced earlier and the things you are experiencing now are they not all fishing?' The boy thought about it and said, 'Yes father, I think they are.' 'My son pull in the nets they are full for you.' The boy pulled in the nets into the boat, expecting them to be overflowing with fish. 'Father there is only enough fish for you and me to live off.' 'My son, have we not caught fish? I thought you wanted to fish?' 'I do father but we should catch loads of fish so we can be rich.' 'My son are you not enjoying the fishing?' 'Yes father but if we were rich, we could be happy!' 'My son, if you were rich would you fish?' 'No father, I would not fish.' 'My son what would you do?' 'I would get other people to fish for me.' 'My son what would you do then?' 'Well, I would sit on the dock and watch them go out to fish.' 'My son, perhaps, you are still a child. It wasn't long ago when you did exactly that and begged me to allow you to fish.' The father turned the boat around and headed home to port. The boy said nothing, he just sat and watched his father steer the boat home. They moored the boat and the boy got out of the boat and as he walked across the jetty he turned around and said to his father, 'Father I know the answer to the question.' 'What is it my son?' 'The preparation in itself is not important, it is part of the experience of fishing. You know it has to be done and you do it willingly, because you love fishing. It is not about the money, it's not about proving anything to anyone, it is simply the fact you love it. You are living the whole experience and loving every second of it. Even when you are hit by stormy seas and the water is breaking over the boat you love it. When you are fearful of failure and might have to turn back or sink, it makes no difference.' 'Why?' 'Because father, you accept that you cannot love fishing without embracing the whole experience, good and bad. 'My son, I think you will make a great fisherman.' The boy laughed, 'I know father, I am your son'."

Pele looked at me and smiled, "I think we are finished Nick. Go fish."

I had grown so fond of Pele and especially our interactions, I was really sad it was over. As I left the office he walked me to the elevator where we shook hands. He said, "Nick, three things to remember." I smiled inside as he said 'three things'. "Live, laugh, love."

A year later , as I stood on the stage receiving my award from Angela for being the company's best salesman, I recalled meeting her for the first time with Pele. As I sat back down, I couldn't help but smile inside, as I thought of Pele. A little voice in my head said, 'Joshua 1:8.'

'Keep this Book of the Law always on your lips; meditate on it day and night, so that you may be careful to do everything written in it. Then you will be prosperous and successful.'

Nick's Notes

Below are some examples of the Art versus the Science of the Spirit of Selling ™

Art	Page	Science	Page
Results versus reasons	15	Know your outcomes or objectives of the call	13
Better thoughts better words better Actions	18	Control - cannot control	16
Your reality is not reality itself just your reality	19	Telling Is Not Selling	19
Rapport is constant but neutral	20	Concrete experience, Observation(internal reflection) Re-apply learning, (adapt to personal context) Do it again (Create new Experience)	25
No Failure only Feedback	23	You cannot NOT communicate	27
Understanding only comes from experience	25	Gaining customer commitment to the next step	29
		Me Us You	43

www.ingramcontent.com/pod-product-compliance
Lightning Source LLC
Chambersburg PA
CBHW020721180526
45163CB00001B/53